Library of
Davidson College

DOING
LEGAL
RESEARCH

APPLIED SOCIAL RESEARCH METHODS SERIES

Series Editors
LEONARD BICKMAN, Peabody College, Vanderbilt University, Nashville
DEBRA J. ROG, Vanderbilt University, Washington, DC

1. **SURVEY RESEARCH METHODS**
   Second Edition
   by FLOYD J. FOWLER, Jr.
2. **INTEGRATING RESEARCH**
   Second Edition
   by HARRIS M. COOPER
3. **METHODS FOR POLICY RESEARCH**
   by ANN MAJCHRZAK
4. **SECONDARY RESEARCH**
   Second Edition
   by DAVID W. STEWART
   and MICHAEL A. KAMINS
5. **CASE STUDY RESEARCH**
   Second Edition
   by ROBERT K. YIN
6. **META-ANALYTIC PROCEDURES FOR SOCIAL RESEARCH**
   Revised Edition
   by ROBERT ROSENTHAL
7. **TELEPHONE SURVEY METHODS**
   Second Edition
   by PAUL J. LAVRAKAS
8. **DIAGNOSING ORGANIZATIONS**
   Second Edition
   by MICHAEL I. HARRISON
9. **GROUP TECHNIQUES FOR IDEA BUILDING**
   Second Edition
   by CARL M. MOORE
10. **NEED ANALYSIS**
    by JACK McKILLIP
11. **LINKING AUDITING AND METAEVALUATION**
    by THOMAS A. SCHWANDT
    and EDWARD S. HALPERN
12. **ETHICS AND VALUES IN APPLIED SOCIAL RESEARCH**
    by ALLAN J. KIMMEL
13. **ON TIME AND METHOD**
    by JANICE R. KELLY
    and JOSEPH E. McGRATH
14. **RESEARCH IN HEALTH CARE SETTINGS**
    by KATHLEEN E. GRADY
    and BARBARA STRUDLER WALLSTON
15. **PARTICIPANT OBSERVATION**
    by DANNY L. JORGENSEN
16. **INTERPRETIVE INTERACTIONISM**
    by NORMAN K. DENZIN
17. **ETHNOGRAPHY**
    by DAVID M. FETTERMAN
18. **STANDARDIZED SURVEY INTERVIEWING**
    by FLOYD J. FOWLER, Jr.
    and THOMAS W. MANGIONE
19. **PRODUCTIVITY MEASUREMENT**
    by ROBERT O. BRINKERHOFF
    and DENNIS E. DRESSLER
20. **FOCUS GROUPS**
    by DAVID W. STEWART
    and PREM N. SHAMDASANI
21. **PRACTICAL SAMPLING**
    by GARY T. HENRY
22. **DECISION RESEARCH**
    by JOHN S. CARROLL
    and ERIC J. JOHNSON
23. **RESEARCH WITH HISPANIC POPULATIONS**
    by GERARDO MARIN
    and BARBARA VANOSS MARIN
24. **INTERNAL EVALUATION**
    by ARNOLD J. LOVE
25. **COMPUTER SIMULATION APPLICATIONS**
    by MARCIA LYNN WHICKER
    and LEE SIGELMAN
26. **SCALE DEVELOPMENT**
    by ROBERT F. DeVELLIS
27. **STUDYING FAMILIES**
    by ANNE P. COPELAND
    and KATHLEEN M. WHITE
28. **EVENT HISTORY ANALYSIS**
    by KAZUO YAMAGUCHI
29. **RESEARCH IN EDUCATIONAL SETTINGS**
    by GEOFFREY MARUYAMA
    and STANLEY DENO
30. **RESEARCHING PERSONS WITH MENTAL ILLNESS**
    by ROSALIND J. DWORKIN
31. **PLANNING ETHICALLY RESPONSIBLE RESEARCH**
    by JOAN E. SIEBER

Other volumes in this series are listed at the end of the book

DOING LEGAL RESEARCH

A Guide for Social Scientists and Mental Health Professionals

Roberta Morris
Bruce D. Sales
Daniel W. Shuman

Applied Social Research Methods Series
Volume 43

SAGE Publications
International Educational and Professional Publisher
Thousand Oaks London New Delhi

Copyright © 1997 by Sage Publications, Inc.

All rights reserved. No part of this book may be reproduced or utilized in any form or by any means, electronic or mechanical, including photocopying, recording, or by any information storage and retrieval system, without permission in writing from the publisher.

For information address:

SAGE Publications, Inc.
2455 Teller Road
Thousand Oaks, California 91320
E-mail: order@sagepub.com

SAGE Publications Ltd.
6 Bonhill Street
London EC2A 4PU
United Kingdom

SAGE Publications India Pvt. Ltd.
M-32 Market
Greater Kailash I
New Delhi 110 048 India

Printed in the United States of America

Library of Congress Cataloging-in-Publication Data

Morris, Roberta A.
   Doing legal research : a guide for social scientists and mental health professionals / authors, Roberta Morris, Bruce D. Sales, and Daniel W. Shuman.
     p.   cm. — (Applied social research methods series ; v. 43)
   Includes bibliographical references and index.
   ISBN 0-8039-3429-7 (pbk.). — ISBN 0-8039-3428-9 (cloth)
    1. Legal research—United States. 2. Mental health personnel—United States—Handbooks, manuals, etc. 3. Social scientists—United States—Handbooks, manuals, etc. I. Sales, Bruce Dennis.
II. Shuman, Daniel, W. III. Title. IV. Series.
KF240.M657   1997
340'.072073—dc20   96-35664

This book is printed on acid-free paper.

97 98 99 00 01 02 10 9 8 7 6 5 4 3 2 1

Production Editor: LaVonne Taylor
Typesetter: Rebecca Evans

Contents

Preface ix

1. **Introduction to Legal Research** 1
   Library Research in Social Sciences and in the Law 3
   General Suggestions About Legal Research 4
   Getting Started 7

2. **Finding Case Law** 14
   Case Reporting Systems 14
   Citation Style 20
   Reading Cases 22
   Finding Other Relevant Cases 25
   Exercises 28
   Answers to Exercises 32
   Appendix 2.1 35
   Appendix 2.2 63

3. **Finding Statutes and Legislative History** 68
   Finding Statutes 68
   Citation Style 75
   Locating Legislative History 76
   Checking the Status of Proposed Legislation 83
   Exercises 84
   Answers to Exercises 87
   Appendix 3.1 89
   Appendix 3.2 98

4. **Finding Administrative Rules, Regulations, Decisions, and Orders** 100
   State-Mandated Public Access to Government Information 100
   Federally Mandated Public Access to Government Information 102

Federal Administrative Law Research Tools—Rules and Regulations	104
Federal Administrative Law Research Tools—Decisions and Orders	107
Citation Style	108
Other Information Sources	109
Exercises	110
Answers to Exercises	112
Appendix 4.1	114
Appendix 4.2	118
Appendix 4.3	120
Appendix 4.4	122
Epilogue	**129**
References	**130**
Supplementary Reading	**132**
Index	**133**
About the Authors	**138**

This book is dedicated to the memory of
Roberta A. Morris. We believe that had she been alive
at its completion, she would have wanted her dedication
to be in loving memory of her mother, Anna C. Morris.

Preface

Social science relevant to legal and public policy issues has emerged as a vital part of such behavioral and social science disciplines as anthropology, criminology, economics, linguistics, philosophy, political science, psychology, and sociology. To develop such work properly, the law and legal issues in question have to be fully identified, understood, and operationalized. This cannot happen unless the social researcher is able to accurately *find* the law. Yet, nowhere in undergraduate or graduate education are there courses or books specifically written to help the nonlaw student or researcher become capable, let alone proficient, in this task. *Doing Legal Research: A Guide for Social Scientists and Mental Health Professionals* is designed to remedy this deficiency.

A similar problem arises for mental health practitioners. Students and practitioners of gerontology, psychology, psychiatric nursing, psychiatry, and social work need to understand the law's mandates on a particular topic to study or practice appropriately. For example, it is common to hear such questions as "What does the law require me to tell patients so to secure 'informed consent to services' in our state?" or "What is the legal standard for finding a person not guilty by reason of insanity in our state?" More and more legal questions are being asked by all mental health practitioners and not just those in forensic mental health practice.

Knowing how to find the law is essential for scientists to develop and execute their research more appropriately and for practitioners to respond more effectively to the difficult challenges that every practice increasingly presents. This text will help these researchers and practitioners to seek answers to pressing legal questions. One cautionary note is important, however: This book is *not* intended to substitute for legal advice from an attorney.

While our primary goal is to aid scientists and practitioners, this volume will also assist prelaw students in becoming more familiar with the basics of legal research prior to entering law school. There is nothing mysterious about learning how to find the law, once appropriate guidance is given. For such students, knowledge of basic legal research skills should accelerate their initial learning curve when they start their formal legal education.

To achieve the above goals, this text provides an easy and understandable format for social science researchers, mental health practitioners, and students to learn this new skill. In addition, to help the reader stay focused on our key purpose—instruction on how to find the law—we have kept the book as brief as possible. Because of this, other relevant topics, such as how to design social science and law research or write a forensic report, are not covered in this volume. Another excluded topic is computer-based legal research methods, such as LEXIS and WESTLAW. To use these services effectively, one needs to first understand the fundamentals of legal research described in this text. Although these computer services are becoming increasingly popular in legal education and practice, subscription costs are prohibitive for nonlawyers. Readers should first learn how to find the law the old-fashioned way—on the library shelves.

BRUCE D. SALES
DANIEL W. SHUMAN

1

Introduction to Legal Research

This book takes the reader into what is unchartered territory for most social scientists and mental health practitioners—the law library. Although legal research skills are often overlooked in behavioral and social science (hereinafter referred to as just social science) training, they are important to scholars and practitioners in this domain.

For researchers, the importance of the law can vary with the issue being investigated. Obviously for many researchers (e.g., most neuroscientists), the law is an irrelevant body of unrelated information. But for many others, it can enrich the scientific process. For some research topics, legal knowledge provides valuable background information about the issue under study. For example, studies on pornography do not necessarily demand an understanding of the legal definition of obscenity or the way criminal law responds to certain sexual behavior, but such information can be important for knowing in advance whether the research will have applied value. Knowledge of certain laws may also influence researchers to revise their independent and dependent variables and measures so that the research has greater external validity.

In many other cases, finding the law can be essential for researchers. For example, studies that attempt to be directly relevant to a wide variety of societal issues often require the researcher to understand the law so to design a valid study of the phenomena. This can be the case with research on sexual harassment, privacy, or virtually any topic of interest to psycholegal, sociolegal, or policy scholars, as well as to scholars studying social issues from a wide variety of disciplines (e.g., anthropology, economics, linguistics, political science, psychology, and sociology). Conversely, the lack of certain legal knowledge can be scientifically problematic. For years, social psychologists have often studied the trial process without any knowledge of the relevant law and legal procedures, relying instead on their familiarity with television dramas of courtroom behavior. The result has been a body of literature that has generally been ignored by the law.

Thus, skills for finding the law will help to ensure the legal relevance of the initial research question and allow researchers to select independent and dependent variables and measures that increase the external validity of their research, by enabling them to conduct their own evaluation of primary legal materials. In addition, these skills allow the researcher to go beyond the more traditional areas of social science-related law research by improving the legal sophistication of such studies and by facilitating the extent to which the researcher can identify certain areas of the law that have not yet been empirically researched.

Practitioners, particularly those in the mental health field, may have a similar need for such information. Using the lessons taught in this book will increase their competence by allowing them to identify the legal mandates applicable to their practice. Knowing the law can help them to keep their practice within legal boundaries and be more attuned to legal advice. Beyond that, many areas of mental health practice are controlled or constrained by the law in specific ways, such as during a forensic evaluation, for which a lack of legal understanding can become very risky. For example, conducting an insanity defense evaluation without knowing the specific legal test for insanity in the case's jurisdiction can result in a legal and ethical challenge to the work of the practitioner. Unfortunately, experience has taught us that lawyers do not always convey this information to the professional whom they have hired.

This text will assist researchers and practitioners in developing their proficiency with legal materials (a) by describing how to use the law library to find, cite, and track cases, statutes passed by state legislatures or Congress, legislative histories of these statutes, and administrative rules, regulations, and decisions promulgated by state and federal administrative agencies (e.g., the Environmental Protection Agency); and (b) by explaining how to use the legal reference systems. In addition, suggested exercises are included at the end of each chapter to increase one's awareness of research questions for which particular skills are necessary, as well as to provide an opportunity to actually use the law library to test one's developing skills on genuine legal questions.

This chapter begins by presenting the differences between library research in the social sciences and that in the law. The chapters that follow offer general information and suggestions about the process of legal research that apply to research questions involving cases (Chapter 2), statutes and legislative history (Chapter 3), and administrative rules, regulations, decisions, and orders (Chapter 4), as well as those questions that do not fit neatly into any one of these categories.

LIBRARY RESEARCH IN SOCIAL SCIENCES AND IN THE LAW

The fact that library research in the social sciences is different from research in the law may not be immediately apparent, unless one is familiar with both disciplines. This difference is subtle yet has significant implications, thus requiring careful consideration and emphasis.

Library research in the social sciences is typically undertaken to prepare a literature review that summarizes existing relevant research, not only to guard against unintentional replication of another's findings but also to demonstrate how the present study supplements and advances prior research. This literature review typically entails an analysis of a single type of reference (i.e., professional journal articles) that has been found by the use of often only one citator, such as the Social Science Citation Index or Psychological Abstracts. Although most literature reviews are intended to be comprehensive, library researchers are allowed a certain measure of discretion in choosing which research to cite. As a result, it is not normally considered a fatal error for researchers if a pertinent study is unintentionally omitted.

By contrast, the purpose of most legal research is to search for the most currently binding legal authority and thus must be more exacting. To accomplish this, it is often necessary to consult federal and state cases and statutes and, where relevant, administrative rules, regulations, decisions, and orders. In addition, the changing nature of the law makes legal research an iterative process in the sense that it is not enough to find, for example, what appear to be the relevant cases. Rather, one must also check each case to make sure that subsequent case decisions, statutes, or regulations have not modified the law in some respect.

This search for the "last word" is the vital distinction between the two disciplines of library research. As a general rule when conducting legal research, social scientists and mental health practitioners must be much more particular about pursuing each and every case, statute, or regulation than need be with citations to relevant empirical studies. However, this does not necessarily mean that they have no discretion whatsoever in choosing legal materials to use as references; it simply means that this discretion must be exercised with greater caution. If controlling law is unintentionally omitted, researchers and practitioners run the risk that their work will become inaccurate or irrelevant.

GENERAL SUGGESTIONS ABOUT LEGAL RESEARCH

The following suggestions should minimize research time and maximize the probability of acquiring complete information on any particular legal topic.

Legal Research Tools

Although the chapters to come are intended to be comprehensive enough for learning how to address most legal research questions, they do not provide an exhaustive coverage of all law library materials. Certain books, such as Jacobstein, Mersky, and Dunn's *Fundamentals of Legal Research* (1994), Price, Bitner, and Bysiewicz's *Effective Legal Research* (1979), and Cohen, Berring, and Olson's *How to Find the Law* (1989), to name some of the better known ones, offer a more exhaustive treatment of the law. These books and others mentioned in the References and Supplementary Reading sections are worth examining but need not be purchased, as they are available in most law libraries.

Every beginning legal researcher will need to purchase a few supplementary legal research tools, however, most of which are inexpensive and available at virtually any law school bookstore. One such tool is *The Bluebook: A Uniform System of Citation* (1996), a paperback published by the Harvard Law Review Association. This book, the legal equivalent of the Publication Manual of the American Psychological Association (APA, 1995), is the authoritative style sheet for legal writing. Other useful acquisitions are Cohen's *Legal Research in a Nutshell* (1992) and Weihofen's *Legal Writing Style* (1980). While they contain most of the information included in the more lengthy tomes, these texts also have the advantage of being succinct and designed for easy reference. For mastering legal language, one should consider purchasing a good law dictionary, such as *Black's Law Dictionary* (Black, 1990).

Law Libraries

Most academic law libraries have all the materials required for basic legal research. Collections in law school libraries range from under 100,000 volumes to over 1,000,000 volumes. Yet, the reality is that, because these libraries' mission is to support the curriculum and re-

INTRODUCTION TO LEGAL RESEARCH

search of its students and faculty, some materials needed for in-depth research in your specific area may only be available on interlibrary loan.

Law libraries may be organized and operated somewhat differently than other libraries that you have used. For instance, not all law libraries are arranged in the same way; there is no universal arrangement of a collection. Most use the Library of Congress classification system at least for text and treatises. A card or on-line catalog will help you find these materials, and written guides or maps are also often available to help you locate materials. If you are unable to locate something that you require quickly, ask a librarian. Often, materials are kept in special collections. For example, all tax and labor law materials at the University of Arizona are shelved together in a separate room; in other libraries, these or other materials (e.g., securities law materials) may be segregated from the main collection and housed together in a separate room or floor of the library. Furthermore, most libraries have a reserve or reference collection stored apart from the main collection. Many libraries with a shortage of space keep some of their materials in storage and only accessible to library employees.

In addition to the problems created by special collections, a law library usually has only a limited collection of federal government publications. These documents are provided under the Depository Library Act that allows Federal Depository Libraries to select one copy of any publication distributed through the program. Only those U.S. publications that best suit the needs of library patrons and the local population are selected. Therefore, many law libraries have as few as 8% of the available documents. If the law library does not have the needed materials, the main or public library may be a federal depository that keeps the needed document. Otherwise, the researcher or practitioner should ask the law librarian to obtain the documents through interlibrary loan. If time is not a factor in obtaining these publications, then many of them can be acquired directly from the U.S. Government Printing Office[1] for a small price.

The greatest resource in a law library will often times be the reference librarians. Their knowledge and assistance may save you hours of time. Take advantage of their expertise.

Attorneys as Research Consultants

There are two reasons why social researchers and mental health practitioners ought to cultivate the acquaintance of several attorneys.

First, law is a diverse field with many specialties and subspecialties, some of which are exceedingly complex. Legal research in these areas will benefit from a brief conference with a legal specialist prior to formalizing the research design. Knowledge gleaned from an attorney can enhance the researcher or practitioner's academic understanding of relevant legal issues.

Second, consulting with a practicing attorney can provide a more accurate idea of the frequency of particular legal situations than simply reading the reported cases. Some legal issues may be more amenable to compromise and settlement prior to trial than others, and this knowledge is almost exclusively an attorney's realm. Moreover, with the exception of federal trial courts and several state courts, only appellate cases are reported and those represent a small fraction of trial court cases. Thus, by using the number of reported cases as an index, the researcher or practitioner may underestimate the frequency with which a specific type of conflict actually occurs. This example underscores the value of an attorney's knowledge, without which a researcher or practitioner could unwittingly reach an erroneous conclusion.

Form Books

Because practicing attorneys face legal situations of a recurring nature, form books are available that contain samples of such commonly used legal documents and instruments as simple wills and contracts; for example, *American Jurisprudence Legal Forms, Second Edition* (1994) and *West's Legal Forms, Revised Second Edition* (Lieberson, 1990). Depending on the particular research goal, these books make useful reference guides because of the information they provide about the kinds of data routinely recorded for different types of legal transactions. The researcher can design research with greater legal sophistication by knowing that certain sources of information are collected as a matter of course. Similarly, there are books of model jury instructions for most states and federal jurisdictions, containing instructions that a judge reads to a jury to guide its behavior during the course of a trial and a judge's deliberations at the end of the trial; for example, *Model Federal Jury Instructions: Criminal & Civil* (Sand, 1984). While these volumes may be more useful to researchers, they also contain information that may assist mental health practitioners as well. In an insanity defense case, for example, jury instructions present how a judge instructs a jury on an applicable law, including the test of insanity.

Primary and Secondary Sources

Cases, statutes, administrative rules, regulations, decisions, and executive documents are legally authoritative and as such are known as *primary* sources. Everything else, including treatises, legal encyclopedias, and legal periodicals (e.g., law reviews), are known as *secondary* source material. Primary sources are the law itself; secondary sources provide indexes, summaries of the law, and comments on the law. Although secondary sources may discuss the law or direct the researcher to primary sources, they are not statements of authoritative law and should *not* be cited as a reference to the law. For instance, never cite a law review article as the source of the law but rather cite the direct primary source—be it a court's opinion, statute, administrative rule or regulation, or executive order. Secondary sources, however, can be cited for their interpretative commentary on the law and for their persuasive value.

GETTING STARTED

The following three chapters divide legal research into neat, discrete segments—case law, statutory law, and administrative rules, regulations, and decisions—but keep in mind that this is for learning purposes only. The answers to legal problems are very rarely found solely by reference to one source of law. It is far more common that complete information about a legal topic can be obtained only by consulting a combination of legal sources in an interactive way. Often, for example, court opinions refer to statutes that refer to pertinent legal history that, in turn, cite agency rules and regulations that, coming full circle, refer to more court decisions. Throughout the upcoming chapters, the same legal research example described at the end of this chapter will be used to illustrate how several different legal sources can be relevant to the same legal issue.

As you learned in high school civics, there are state and federal governments, each composed of executive, legislative, and judicial branches. Although their authority is equal in theory, it is hierarchical in practice. Finding and understanding the law requires a knowledge of this hierarchy. In general, in areas where the federal government is empowered to act by the federal constitution (e.g., interstate commerce, federal taxation, national defense, and foreign relations), federal law prevails over conflicting state law. In areas where the federal government is not constitutionally empowered to act (e.g., local zoning, marital relations, and property succession), state or local (county or city) law prevails over conflicting federal law. While this division of authority is clear at the far ends of the spectrum, the line drawn in close cases has been the subject of much controversy.

Within the state or federal government, the executive, legislative, and judicial branches derive their equal authority from the state or federal constitution. Although we may have been taught that legislatures make the law, executive branches enforce it, and courts interpret it, comprehensive legal research requires a recognition of their interrelated functions in making law. The actions of the legislative branch that enact statutes, the executive branch that implement them through rulemaking and case-by-case decisions, and the courts that apply and interpret them, as well as make decisions in the absence of statutes or regulations—are all sources of law. A court's interpretation of a statute or regulation is subject to subsequent action by the legislative or executive branches that amend or repeal that statute or rule to achieve a different result. An executive branch agency's administrative regulation that interprets a statute or implements a court decision is subject to the court's analysis of the rule or the legislature's action.

In the following chapters, we will assume that the researcher or practitioner has already obtained the first citation to a case, statute, or administrative rule or regulation. For this reason, it is necessary to explain here exactly how one goes about getting that indispensable first cite.

There are several ways to begin research on a legal topic, none of which are necessarily preferable to any other. The easiest way, of course, is for someone to provide you with a statute or a case on point. With this information, you can go directly to that source of law. If this is not the case, then the following alternative methods are available, listed in descending order with respect to their ease of use and completeness of coverage.

Treatises or Texts

One of the best sources for finding initial citations is a treatise or text. Generally, it covers one area of law and discusses the rules and principles of law along with commentary on and analysis of the subject area. In a similar vein, the social science researcher or mental health practitioner (hereinafter referred to as simply the legal researcher or beginning legal researcher) can consult any of the following: (a) multivolume treatises on various subjects, some of which are written by highly respected legal commentators and present scholarly treatments of the issues; and (b) *restatements* of the law that are model laws with commentary covering many legal areas, published under the auspices of the American Law Institute.

Law Reviews

Another easy source for finding these initial citations are relevant law review articles that typically provide complete information on the legal topic under consideration. To do this, locate the topic in one of the several indexes to legal periodicals. The primary ones are the Current Law Index (C.L.I.)-Legal Resource Index (L.R.I.) and the Index to Legal Periodicals (I.L.P.).

The C.L.I.-L.R.I. is the most comprehensive and is produced both as a print service (C.L.I.) and on microfilm or CD-ROM (L.R.I.). Online access is available on LEXIS and WESTLAW, to be discussed later. L.R.I. provides a listing of over 700 law and law-related journals, and several legal newspapers. It is subdivided into a subject index, author and title index, table of cases, table of statutes, and a list of publications indexed and is totally cumulated every month. According to the publisher, quarterly cumulations are also available March, June, and September. This allows you to search only one source instead of consulting several volumes. C.L.I. contains a subject index and an author and title index. Full bibliographic information is provided under both subject and author, as well as case and statute tables. The author and title index offers only titles of reviewed books, not titles of articles. The only drawback of C.L.I.-L.R.I. is its newness—it only covers materials dating from 1980. For earlier materials, I.L.P. must be used.

I.L.P. covers over 600 legal periodicals. It is organized into subdivisions, with a subject and author index, table of cases, table of statutes, and book review index. It is a print service published monthly except in September and includes a bound cumulative copy issued each year. Hence, I.L.P. is not only less comprehensive than C.L.I.-L.R.I. but also more difficult to use, because it is only cumulated within each year rather than across the total data base.

Depending on the topic, the use of these indexes should turn up a number of citations to relevant law review articles. In addition, unless one is already well versed in the intricacies of the specific legal topic, reading these articles is often an extremely useful starting point—more so than reading a particular case or statute—because they generally provide an overview of the topic by analyzing the relevant law and discussing the salient issues.

Legal Encyclopedias

A third method is to use a legal encyclopedia, such as *Corpus Juris Secundum* (C.J.S.), *American Jurisprudence 2d*[2] (Am. Jur. 2d), or *American Law Reports* (A.L.R.), to find a review of the subject. Although the articles themselves are not highly regarded in academic circles, they are a useful research tool because they set forth principles of law along with extensive footnotes that contain hundreds of citations to relevant cases and statutes.

These textual services also provide other relevant information. For example, the A.L.R. system publishes a small selection of state appellate court decisions. Although it does not provide the comprehensive coverage of the West system (described in the next chapter) in terms of the sheer number of cases reported, it does provide an in-depth analysis of the cases that it publishes, by including extensive editorial annotations that are periodically updated to reflect current trends in the law. These annotations are just as useful a tool as an encyclopedia or law review article for finding additional citations to relevant cases. Like the West system, the A.L.R. series is periodically renumbered and accessed by a digesting system, described below.

In addition to the West series, Lawyers Co-op, which publishes A.L.R. and the *Lawyer's Edition of the U.S. Supreme Court Reports,* also publishes the *American Law Reports-Federal* (A.L.R.-Fed.) that contains a limited selection of annotated federal cases. This selection is small compared to the West series and not recommended for comprehensive searches, even though the annotations are useful. Lawyers Co-op also publishes a digest series for these materials, the *American Law Reports Digest* and *American Law Reports-Federal Digest* to be used respectively with the A.L.R. and A.L.R.-Fed.

Restatements of Law

The American Law Institute is an organization composed of distinguished judges, lawyers, and law professors elected to its membership. The Institute's primary purpose is to provide systematic *restatements* of case law on select topics. These restatements are written by leading authorities working in committees and subject to the approval of the Institute's membership. Various drafts of them are discussed at annual conferences and revised several times before they are finally approved. Although the Institute's work is highly cited, some have criticized it for stating what the law ought to be rather than reporting the majority rule in this country. Nevertheless, it is an excellent source for learning about specific legal topics and finding relevant, key citations to cases and statutes. The restatements can be found in all law libraries.

Law Digests

A final general source for locating initial citations are the subject indexes that appear with most statutory compilations and law digests. Statutes, created by legislatures as session laws (passed during the recent session of the legislature) are organized by subject into a series of state and federal volumes known as a statutory code or compilation. The subject index to these volumes provides easy access to such materials.

A corresponding method for finding initial case citations is to use digests, essentially indexing systems for cases. Although specific digest systems will be described in the next chapter, a discussion of their mechanics is included here to illustrate their usefulness for finding these citations.

Digests are an essential research tool, because cases are not published by subject or topic but in chronological order. Digests contain an alphabetical arrangement of legal topics and subtopics. Under each subtopic are citations to the relevant cases and brief summaries of the points of law for which they are authority. The citations are also accompanied by references to statutes, rules and regulations, or legislative history considered by the court to be directly relevant. A set of digests also includes volumes other than those that order the cases by subject. For example, there are volumes of case names—in the event that you have the name but no cite—and volumes of descriptive words in case you know the issue but not the case name or citation. Finally, many digests contain sets of "Words and Phrases," dictionary-like volumes that refer the reader to primary sources that define or construe particular terms and phrases that have legal significance.

The comprehensiveness of these digests allows a researcher or practitioner to approach a question with a high degree of particularity from several different angles. For example, terms derived from an analysis of legal concepts involved (e.g., legal theories, such as breach of contract, trespass, or negligence) and from an assessment of the parameters of the factual situation (e.g., the parties, the place where the incident occurred, and mitigating circumstances) can be used to locate cases. One drawback to this method, however, is the possibility of searching a great number of narrow index terms with little success in finding relevant cases. Furthermore, the case summaries are often so brief that it becomes difficult to determine whether a specific case is actually on point or only tangentially related to the research issue. Therefore, these digests should never replace reading a case itself. Such drawbacks can make a digest search a less efficient method than the prior techniques (e.g., treatise and text) for coming up with the initial case citations needed to research a topic. Once a single relevant case has been obtained, however, the specific index terms become apparent and the digest search becomes efficient and manageable.

One final point: These digests are continually updated with supplementary paperback volumes and "pocketparts"—supplements that slip into the back cover of the main hardbound volume. After consulting the main volumes, check the supplements for the most recent cases.

Computer-Assisted Research

A considerable amount of legal research normally conducted by combing through stacks of books can also be managed at a computer terminal. Services such as those offered by LEXIS and WESTLAW are extremely useful, but the beginning legal researcher should only use them after gaining a thorough understanding of the legal materials as they exist in their print form. The reasoning behind this is simple: every law library has books available to the public, but the cost of computer services may be prohibitive and you may not always have easy access to them.

Knowing When to Stop

In addition to establishing a routine for starting the research process, a researcher or practitioner also needs to develop a feel for knowing when to stop researching the issue. Specific techniques for checking whether the last judicial, legislative, or administrative word has been found are described in the following chapters. It is much more difficult, however, to determine whether the researcher or practitioner has gained a comprehensive overview of all the relevant legal issues. The best that can be suggested is that the following questions be asked:

- Does any of the research indicate a statutory or constitutional basis for the decision, and if so, have those statutes or constitutional provisions been examined?
- In addition to the statutes themselves, has their relevant legal history (i.e., their interpretation by the courts) been analyzed?
- Is there relevant case law from the state courts on this issue?
- Is this a legal topic where the state courts and the federal courts share jurisdiction? Have the federal materials also been consulted?
- Is it possible that such determinations would also be made by administrative agencies? Have these materials been examined?
- Are there corresponding state or local laws that duplicate an existing federal legal scheme in some respect? Have these materials been analyzed?

NOTES

1. Superintendent of Documents, Government Printing Office, Washington, D.C. 20402.
2. 2d refers to the second edition.

2

Finding Case Law

When a dispute arises between parties that they have not been able to resolve between themselves or with the assistance of a mediator, they often have the opportunity to take their claims to a court. The court then has the responsibility of resolving the dispute in light of the relevant law (i.e., constitutional law, statutory law, prior case law, or administrative rules, regulations, and decisions or a combination thereof). The party who loses then has an opportunity to appeal the decision to a higher or appellate court. These court decisions play an important role in our legal system because of the doctrine of precedent or *stare decisis*. Simply stated, *stare decisis* means that a rule of law announced by an appellate court is binding on all lower courts in that jurisdiction. Because of this, lawyers spend a great deal of time conducting legal research to find judicial opinions dealing with issues presented by the cases that they are working on.

This chapter starts with the assumption that the reader has obtained at least one case citation, using the methods previously described. With this citation as a starting point, this chapter describes the federal and state case reporting systems, the correct citation style for cases, the necessary steps to find the full text of opinions, a method for extracting the most useful information from opinions, and how to use this information to find other relevant cases. A state case, *Reed v. State* (*v.* stands for versus), will be used to illustrate certain points. An edited version of this opinion is included in Appendix 2.1 for easy reference. We selected this case, because it deals with an issue that has been of interest to both social science researchers and mental health practitioners—the use of polygraphy.

CASE REPORTING SYSTEMS

State Decision

All states have trial courts where a case is first heard and at least one appellate court that reviews the trial court's decision if one of the parties is dissatisfied with it and wants to pursue an appeal. In most states, appeals go directly to an intermediate appellate court. If one of the parties is still dissatisfied, then he or she can submit an appeal to the state's supreme court. Some states, however, do not have an intermediate appellate court. In these jurisdictions (e.g., Maine and Mississippi), an appeal from a trial court goes directly to the state's supreme court, because it is the only appellate court. States usually establish their court systems in their constitutions or by statute. Check to determine the structure of a particular state's court system.

Generally, state trial courts (e.g., the Superior Courts in Arizona) do not publish their court decisions. The exceptions are Pennsylvania, Ohio, and New York, where some trial court opinions are published. On the other hand, court opinions are written and published for all state appellate courts. Those states with more than one level of appellate court usually publish the decisions of the intermediate appellate courts in a separate series from the state's highest appellate court (typically referred to as the state's supreme court). Ohio, for example, publishes opinions of the Ohio Court of Appeals in the *Ohio Appellate Reports* and opinions of the Ohio Supreme Court in *Ohio State Reports*.

These opinions are published in official or unofficial reports (a compendium of the reported opinions published chronologically) or both. Official law reports are published by each state's government or by a private publisher under a grant of authority from the legislature as evidenced in a state statute. For example, the Nebraska Supreme Court opinions are published in a series called *Nebraska Reports* that are published by the State of Nebraska. The opinions of the Arizona Supreme Court are published in a series called *Arizona Reports* that are published by West Publishing Company, a private publisher under the authority of the Arizona legislature. This authority is documented in state legislation, in this case *Arizona Revised Statutes Annotated* Section 12-108 (1982).

Those states (including the District of Columbia) that do not have official reporters rely on the *unofficial* regional reporter systems (described below) to publish opinions from their highest courts. Unofficial reports are published by a private publisher without legislative authority. Some states have discontinued official reporter systems, because of the cost and the fact that the unofficial reporter systems—primarily the West *National Reporter* (West) system—often publishes the opinions more quickly. In addition, these unofficial reporter systems often provide invaluable supplementary information and analysis not given in the state reporters and also supply a consistent form of case analysis that serves a unifying function across states. It is obviously easier and more efficient to use one or two indexing systems for all legal research needs than to use 50. A list of the key official and unofficial reporters for the federal cases and the state supreme court cases appears in Appendix 2.2.[1]

The West system, the preferred and most commonly used unofficial reporter, divides the country into seven regions: Atlantic,[2] North Eastern,[3] South Eastern,[4] Southern,[5] South Western,[6] North Western,[7] and Pacific[8] with separate sets of volumes published for each of these regions. Each set contains most of the cases decided by the appellate courts of the states included in that region. In addition, West publishes two separate reporters for the two most litigious states, New York (*New York Supplement*) and California (*California Reporter*).

The West system distributes the opinions quickly by printing them first as pamphlets called *advance sheets* that are circulated before they become part of a bound volume. To prevent the number of volumes in each set from becoming unmanageable, they are periodically renumbered according to series. For example, after the 200th volume of the *Southern Reporter,* West begins the *Southern Reporter, 2nd Series* that starts over with Volume 1. These publications are held together by the all-encompassing West key number indexing and digesting scheme described in greater detail below.

Federal Decisions

Although there are courts of special jurisdiction, such as the U.S. Tax Court, the general outline of the federal courts is a three-tiered hierarchy. The lowest level of the hierarchy contains the trial courts of general jurisdiction, the 97 U.S. District Courts. Each state has at least one federal district court, while the more populous states have several. An appeal from a district court ruling goes to the U.S. Circuit Court of Appeals in the circuit in which the district court is located. As shown in Table 2.1, each circuit covers a multistate area.

These 13 circuit courts of appeals constitute the second tier of federal courts. Finally, an appeal from a circuit court may be heard by the U.S. Supreme Court that sits at the pinnacle of the federal judicial hierarchy.

Opinions of the U.S. Supreme Court are published by three reporters: the official *United States Reports*; West's *Supreme Court Reporter* that incorporates the key number digest system; and Lawyers Co-operative's *Lawyer's Edition of the U.S. Supreme Court Reports* that summarizes the counsels' arguments and provides case annotations. These services are

Table 2.1
Composition of the 13 Federal Judicial Circuits

Circuit	Composition
District of Columbia	District of Columbia
First	Maine, Massachusetts, New Hampshire, Puerto Rico, Rhode Island
Second	Connecticut, New York, Vermont
Third	Delaware, New Jersey, Pennsylvania, Virgin Islands
Fourth	Maryland, North Carolina, South Carolina, Virginia, West Virginia
Fifth	District of the Canal Zone, Louisiana, Mississippi, Texas
Sixth	Kentucky, Michigan, Ohio, Tennessee
Seventh	Illinois, Indiana, Wisconsin
Eighth	Arkansas, Iowa, Minnesota, Missouri, Nebraska, North Dakota, South Dakota
Ninth	Alaska, Arizona, California, Idaho, Montana, Nevada, Oregon, Washington, Guam, Hawaii
Tenth	Colorado, Kansas, New Mexico, Oklahoma, Utah, Wyoming
Eleventh	Alabama, Florida, Georgia
Federal	All federal judicial districts

updated by advance sheets, until the next volume is issued. In addition, there is *U.S. Law Week*,[9] (U.S.L.W.) and the *Supreme Court Bulletin* (S.C.B.), unofficial loose-leaf services that publish the text of the opinions within 24 hours after they are released then deliver them to its subscribers within a week's time. These two services also publish general court information, such as court calendars, dockets, arguments, and motions.

By contrast, there is no official reporter for the lower federal courts. For coverage, lawyers rely on West's *Federal Reporter* for decisions by the U.S. Court of Appeals, West's *Federal Supplement* for decisions by the U.S. District Courts,[10] and West's *Federal Rules Decisions* for federal cases involving procedural matters. These West series also have digests that use the same indexing system as the one that appears with the West state materials.

Although the West federal series is comprehensive, it is not exhaustive. Increasingly, the federal courts are issuing unpublished opinions to deal with their burgeoning work load. By either rendering summary orders or unpublished opinions for those cases that the courts consider to have little precedential value, they hope to dispose of cases more rapidly and spend more time crafting the more important opinions for publication. For discussions of the implications of this policy of "depublication," see Dunn (1977), Gerstein (1984), Reynolds and Richman (1978), and Shuchman and Gelfand (1980).

In general, this procedure does not pose a problem for legal research, because the general policy is that these opinions have no authority as precedent. There is an exception to this general rule, however. Imagine that you have a district court case that was appealed to the circuit court and that the circuit court vacated the district court's opinion and remanded the case.[11] It is at that point, as you search unsuccessfully for this second district court opinion, that you realize that perhaps the opinion was not published or that the parties entered into a consent decree.[12] The only solution to this problem is to call or write to the Clerk of the Court or to the attorneys for information about the final resolution of the case.

Finally, there are unofficial reporters that gather cases together by subject, such as Commerce Clearing House's (C.C.H.) *Labor Cases,* Bureau of National Affairs (B.N.A.) *Environmental Law Reporter,* and West's *Education Law Reporter.* These compendiums are extensive and helpful, because cases can be found easily through the use of the subject indexes.

Digests

Since most case reporters are arranged chronologically and not by subject, legal researchers typically turn to the West digests, each of which is arranged alphabetically by topic from *Abandoned and Lost Property* to *Zoning*. The popular West Key Number System divides law alphabetically into over 400 broad topics, each one then divided into subdivisions, each with a key number. There may be one or two or hundreds of key numbers for a given topic, depending on the legal principles within the scope of that topic. To illustrate, there are more than 300 subtopics for "Constitutional Law," including "Right to use streets" (#134), "Nature of retrospective laws" (#187), and "Liberty to contract" (#89). Under each subtopic are case citations, along with a one-sentence description (or squib) of the cases, and references to statutes, rules, and regulations or legislative history considered by the court or both. Given the topic (e.g., "Constitutional Law") and the key number (e.g., #134), you can then proceed on your search for the relevant cases. Keep in mind that knowing the key number alone is not sufficient. You need both the topic and key number, because all topics start the key numbers from number 1.

If you do not have the name of the case on your point of law, go to the descriptive word index of the digest. Using the most appropriate word or phrase (e.g., mental health), you will find all the relevant topics (e.g., guardians), subtopics (e.g., appointment of a temporary guardian), and the relevant key numbers.

An alternative approach when you know the appropriate topic is to use the "Topic Analysis" within the relevant West digest. The Topic Analysis is similar to a detailed table of contents for a book. It occurs at the beginning of each topic and will list all the key numbers on that topic.

If you know the citation to a case—what lawyers call the one good case—your search for relevant cases on a particular topic is greatly simplified. You can go directly to the relevant West Reporter and find the case where it has the relevant topics and key numbers listed in the beginning of the reported opinion. If you only have the name of the case, you can go to the "Table of Cases" part of the digest that lists cases alphabetically and find the case's citation. Also listed is the history of the case and the topics and key numbers relevant to your case. If you do not have the plaintiff's name but know the defendant's name, many digests have a "Defendant/Plaintiff Table." For example, if the case is *Smithy v. Comer,* you can look up Comer in this table and find the full case name.

Finally, there are volumes of "Words and Phrases," dictionary-like volumes that refer to primary sources that define or construe particular terms. For example, if the purpose of the research is to locate California cases in which the court defined or construed the phrase *mental suffering,* the researcher or practitioner can consult Volume 50 of West's *California Digest 2d* and find those cases listed in which the California courts have considered this topic.

Digests are published by West Publishing Company for use with its state, regional, and federal case reporting systems. For example, West publishes a key number digest (e.g., *California Digest*) for most of the states, four regional digests (i.e., *Atlantic Digest, North Western Digest, Pacific Digest,* and *South Eastern Digest*), and digests for certain courts (e.g., the U.S. Supreme Court, the U.S. Court of Appeals, or all reported cases in the federal district courts). In addition to separate digests, West also publishes the *American Digest System* (A.D.S.), a compilation of the citations for all published state and federal cases—from 1658 to date! The A.D.S. simplifies the research process when citations from across the United States are of more interest than those from just one region. The indexing for the A.D.S. is provided in digests called the *Century Digests* for the early years and, beginning with 1897, in ten-year segments called *Decennial Digests*. These are periodically renumbered (e.g., *First Decennial Digest* covers 1897 to 1906, the *Second Decennial Digest* goes from 1907-1916), thus preventing the series from becoming unmanageable and requiring frequent revision. Since 1976, *Decennial Digests* are now issued in two parts, Part 1 covering the first five years and Part 2 the second. For example, *Ninth Decennial Digest: Part 1* covers 1976 through 1980, while *Ninth Decennial Digest: Part 2* covers 1981 through 1985. The A.D.S. is supplemented by bound volumes called *The General Digest*.

CITATION STYLE

Once you are ready to summarize the results of legal research in written form, the proper citation style must be considered. Cases are cited by the names of the parties underscored (e.g., *Reed v. State*), usually with the plaintiff or the appellant (the party who brings the appeal of the lower court case) coming first. Next comes the location of the court's opinion in the official reporter, if there is one. This part of the citation contains the volume number of the reporter, the abbreviation for the name of the reporter, and the first page number of the opinion. Then comes the location(s) of the opinion in the unofficial reporters, such as the West system. Finally in parentheses, the name of the deciding court is presented, unless it is apparent from the official reporter citation and the year that the decision was rendered. In addition, if the state has an official reporter, the proper citation form places the official citation in front of any unofficial citations to the case. Thus for *Reed,* the citation to *Maryland Reports* precedes the citations to West's *Atlantic Reporter;* for example, *Reed v. State,* 283 Md. 374, 391 A.2d 364 (1978).

As already noted, a proper citation form also requires that the deciding court always be listed. The manner by which this is done varies, depending on which court rendered the decision and whether the state has an official state reporter. In Maryland, for example, the highest court is the Court of Appeals and the intermediate appellate court is the Court of Special Appeals. Assume for a moment that you want to refer to the

Maryland Court of Special Appeals' earlier decision in *Reed* rather than the Maryland Court of Appeals' decision. The correct citation for that decision will read *Reed v. State,* 35 Md. App. 472, 372 A.2d 243 (1977). The difference reflects the fact that it was the decision of the state's intermediate appellate court rather than that of the highest appellate court. In this situation, it is not necessary to specify the deciding court in the parentheses with the date (i.e., Md. 1978)—unless noted otherwise, it is assumed to be the state supreme court or highest appellate court.

Now assume that you want to refer to the Maryland Court of Appeals' decision and that Maryland does not have an official reporter. The correct citation to *Reed* would then become *Reed v. State,* 391 A.2d 364 (Md. 1978). For the decision of the intermediate court of appeals, the correct citation would be 372 A.2d 243 (Md. Ct. Spec. App. 1977). To state the rule more generally, if you only have a citation to an unofficial reporter for a case rendered by a state supreme court or highest state appellate court, you need only to refer to the state in the parentheses with the date. Reference to the state, without any additional information, creates the assumption that it was the state supreme court or highest state appellate court that handed down the decision.

Let us go back now and reconsider what we know from the actual *Reed* citation, *Reed v. State,* 283 Md. 374, 391 A.2d 364 (1978):

1. Because the state is involved, there is reason to believe that it may be a criminal case.[13]
2. Assuming that it is a criminal case, we notice that the defendant's name appears first, indicating that he or she must be appealing from an adverse lower court decision, because at the original trial it would appear as *State v. Reed.*
3. Maryland has an official state reporter.
4. The opinion also appears in the West regional reporter, Volume 391, of the *Atlantic Reporter, Second Series,* starting at page 364.
5. The deciding court was an intermediate appellate court rather than the state supreme court.
6. The case was decided in 1978.
7. Hence, to find the text of an opinion, all one needs to do is locate the section of the library housing the case reporters and select the desired volume of the specific reporter.

The citation system for federal cases is essentially the same in form as it is for the state cases: first the volume number of the reporter, then the abbreviation for the reporter, then the first page number of the opinion, followed in parentheses by the name of the deciding court (e.g., 1st Cir., unless it was the Supreme Court) and the year. For example, *Keller v. State Bar of California,* 496 U.S. 1 (1989) is a case that was decided by the U.S. Supreme Court and appears in Volume 496 of the *United States Reports.* The case starts on the first page of this volume and was decided in 1989.

As already noted, Appendix 2.2 contains the abbreviations for the commonly used state and federal legal materials in this area. For a more extensive discussion of the official state and federal case citation forms in every conceivable situation, see *The Bluebook: A Uniform System of Citation* (1996).

Finding Alternative Citations

In the event that only one citation to a case is known, there are several methods for finding alternative citations. One method is to find the case name in the Table of Cases volume of the appropriate West Digest, where it lists both the official and unofficial citations. Another strategy is to use *Shepard's Citation* (see *infra*) that lists alternative citations in parentheses under the initial citation, as well as presenting citations to subsequent cases where the initial case is cited. Finally, West publishes a text specifically for this purpose, titled the *National Reporter Blue Book.*

READING CASES

Having used a citation to locate the case, there are many lessons to learn about reading a case to extract its essential elements. We will use the court's opinion in *Reed,* as it appears in the West regional reporter, as an example (see Appendix 2.1).

Certain pieces of information are found in every opinion, whether state or federal, in particular places in the opinion. Using the *Reed* case, the following is the information found in the *Atlantic Reporter:*

1. Citation to the official reporter if different from the regional reporter: 283 Md. 374.
2. Names of the parties: James Reed, Jr. v. State of Maryland.
3. Docket number of the case given by the court: No. 62.
4. Court that heard the case: Court of Appeals of Maryland.

FINDING CASE LAW 23

5. Date of the decision: Sept. 6, 1978.
6. Brief unofficial (prepared by West, not the court) synopsis or summary of the case, including the holding (the legal term for that statement containing the actual decision), the judge's name who presented the opinion of the court, and the names of concurring and dissenting judges.

    Defendant was convicted in the Circuit Court, Montgomery County, John F. McAuliffe, J., of rape, unnatural and perverted sex acts, robbery, verbal threats, and unlawful use of the telephone, and he appealed. The Court of Appeals, 35 Md. App. 472, 372 A.2d 243, affirmed. On certiorari, the Court of Appeals, Eldridge, J., held that testimony based on "voiceprints" or spectrograph is inadmissible in Maryland courts as evidence of voice identification because, at the present time, such technique has not reached the required standard of acceptance in the scientific community.

    Reversed and remanded with directions.

    Smith, J., dissented and filed opinion in which Murphy, C. J., and Orth, J., concurred. (p. 364)

7. West key numbers and Headnotes. For example:

    2. Criminal Law (key #)388

    Fairness to litigant requires that before results of a scientific process can be used against him, he is entitled to a scientific judgment of the reliability of that process (p. 364).

8. Attorneys representing the parties.

    William T. Wood, Specially Assigned Public Defender, Rockville, for appellant.

    Deborah K. Handel, Asst. Atty. Gen. (Francis B. Burch, Atty. Gen. and Clarence W. Sharp, Asst. Atty. Gen., Baltimore, on brief) for appellee.

9. Judges sitting for the case.

    Argued before MURPHY, C. J., and SMITH, DIGGES, LEVINE, ELDRIDGE and ORTH, JJ.

    Reargued before MURPHY, C. J., and SMITH, DIGGES, LEVINE, ELDRIDGE, ORTH and COLE, JJ (p. 364).

10. Judge writing the opinion of the majority: Eldridge.
11. Text of the majority opinion: pp. 364-377.
12. Names of judges concurring in the majority opinion, if any: none.
13. Names of judges writing separate concurring opinions, if any: none.
14. Text of the concurring opinions, if any: none.
15. Names of judges writing dissenting opinions, if any: Smith.
16. Text of the dissenting opinions: pp. 377-428.
17. Names of judges concurring in the dissenting opinion: Murphy and Orth.

Several of the above listed items are particularly useful, such as the date of the decision (#5) and the names of the attorneys (#8). For example, in *Reed,* the case was appealed, with the result that the appellate court vacated the lower court's opinion and remanded the case. The second opinion of the lower court was unpublished. To find out how the lower court decided the issues, the deciding court or the attorneys can be contacted for a copy of the opinion. The *Martindale-Hubbell Law Directory* lists the addresses and phone numbers of all practicing attorneys. This directory is usually found in the reference section of most law libraries.

The West key numbers and the accompanying one-sentence descriptive headnotes are also extremely useful. In the previous chapters, we mentioned that if a researcher or practitioner does not already have a case, then merely consulting the digests without some idea of which specific key numbers to use can be an inefficient use of research time. Knowing even one relevant case, however, provides access to the specific key numbers under which similarly pertinent cases will be indexed.

As mentioned above, the *holding* is the critical statement of controlling law that decides the case. Everything else is referred to as *dicta* (plural for *obiter dictum,* meaning "a remark by the way"). Dicta are collateral statements that discuss the legal issues, such as comments in passing, or observations made in analyzing the issue but that stop short of deciding the case. Although it sounds tricky to pick out exactly which of the court's numerous statements is *the* controlling statement of law, another handy legal convention makes it quite simple. Just look for a sentence that includes the words "we hold . . ."; if it is there in the opinion, this is the holding. For example, in *Reed,* the holding is on page 377:

> Thus, based on our examination of the record in the instant case, the judicial opinions that have considered this question, and the available legal and scientific commentaries, we do not believe that "voiceprint" analysis has achieved the general acceptance in the scientific community, at this time, that is required under *Frye.* We therefore hold that testimony based on "voiceprints" or spectrograms is, for the present, inadmissible in Maryland courts as evidence of voice identification. This holding is, of course, subject to reconsideration by the Court if the use of spectrograms or some other technique of voice identification does in the future achieve the general acceptance of the scientific and legal communities.

Besides the satisfaction of finding the definitive legal statement in a case, there is another reason for picking out such mysterious legal language that can be subtle, hence not immediately obvious to many social scientists and mental health practitioners. Let us assume that a researcher is conducting empirical research that examines an issue raised in a court's opinion. When discussing the implications of the law, the researcher should insert a direct quote of the court's holding in the case rather than a paraphrase. A similar approach would hold true for the mental health practitioner when writing an assessment report that refers to the law's test (such as that for the imposition of a guardianship) that guided the practitioner's evaluation. Because the particular language the court used is *the* statement of controlling law, many attorneys prefer to read the court's language verbatim—particularly the holding—rather than someone else's interpretation. This is not to say that comments on the implications of court decisions or speculations on directions in which the law seems to be moving are inappropriate, but rather that the exact language of the court should be included along with the analysis.

Finally, the value of *briefing* cases needs to be considered.[14] Briefing involves writing a brief summary of the case, including a description of the facts, a statement of the legal issues decided by the court, a succinct sentence or two about the court's underlying rationale for the decision, and the holding itself. Writing case briefs is a good exercise for the beginning legal researcher, because it helps to develop the ability to pick out the most important aspects of a case. It is also excellent for the more advanced legal researcher, as the important element of the case becomes available for subsequent easy reference.

FINDING OTHER RELEVANT CASES

Citations found in the initial case can be used to locate additional relevant cases, and reading them will enrich the researcher or practitioner's understanding of the issues, as well as lead to other related case citations found in the body of these other opinions.

The West key numbers located at the beginning of the initial case (headnotes) also can be used to locate other citations to cases. As previously noted, you can take the topic and key number relevant to your subject of interest to any West digest and find all of the cases indexed under that topic and key number in that digest. For example, headnote 6 in the *Reed* case uses the key number "Criminal Law key no. 339.6" that incorporates the topic of whether voiceprints or spectrographs are admissible in Maryland courts. By taking Criminal Law 339.6 to the *Arizona Digest,* you can find out if any Arizona cases have ruled on this issue. By taking it to the *American Digest System,* you can find any other cases, both federal and state, on this particular subject.

Finally, another method of finding other relevant cases is to use *Shepard's Citations*. The initial case citation can be *Shepardized* to discover whether subsequent decisions have modified the holding in any respect and whether it has been cited in any subsequent cases that may be on point. *Shepardizing* is a research technique unique to the law. When used as a verb, it refers to the process of consulting the *Shepard's Citations* volumes for the complete citation history and treatment of the case by other courts.[15] The primary purpose of consulting *Shepard's Citations* is to "bring the case up to date." *Shepard's* will indicate if the case has been affirmed, modified, or reversed on appeal. In addition, *Shepard's* will indicate how your case has been treated in subsequent decisions of the same court (e.g., followed, criticized, limited, questioned, or overruled). Thus, a case must always be *Shepardized* to ensure that it is still good law and has not been overturned or modified by a subsequent decision.

There are separate *Shepard's Citations* for every state, regional, federal, and Supreme Court reporter, as well as for all statutes and some administrative agency rulings and law review articles. *Shepard's Citations* are supplemented by bound volumes and paper pamphlets. You must always check each primary bound volume, each supplemental bound volume, and each pamphlet. The last pamphlet will indicate on its front cover what prior volumes should also be checked.

For example, if the *Reed* case were to be *Shepardized,* then the *Shepard's* volume(s) containing the citation for the *Atlantic Reporter, 2d Series,* Volume 391, page 364, would be used. The first citation appearing under the page number, 283 Md. 374 in parentheses, is the alternative to the official reporter. It is followed by another citation in parentheses, 97 ALR 201, that is the *Atlantic Reporter* citation to the same case. By consulting the supplements as well as the main volume, it can be observed that *Reed* has been cited in many cases throughout the United States since it was decided in 1978.

The lower-case letters appearing to the left of some of the subsequently listed cases provide additional information about the cited case, such as whether it followed the holding in *Reed* (f), overruled it (o), or modified it (m). The small numerical superscripts appearing immediately to the left of the page number in some of the citations refer to the paragraph with the corresponding number in the original case opinion. These superscripts indicate that the subsequent opinion has cited the earlier opinion because of the points made in the particular numbered paragraph in this earlier opinion. For example, the fourth paragraph of the *Reed* case has been followed by the subsequent case that appears at 394 A.2d 1216. Thus, if the goal of the research is to locate subsequent cases that use the earlier case as authority for only certain points, then these numbers enable the legal researcher to conduct this very specific search. The complete explanation of the symbol system, along with an illustration, appears in the front of each *Shepard's* volume.

The citations found for the *Reed* case in *Shepard's* need to be examined to determine why *Reed* was cited in these cases. Although it seems safe to assume that *Reed* was cited with respect to the admissibility of evidence obtained from some relatively new scientific method, the particular method with which these subsequent courts wrestled may not have been voice spectrography as was the case in *Reed*. Using the *Shepard's* listing and reviewing the cases cited by *Shepard's* reveals that *Reed* was cited in cases dealing with the scientific admissibility of evidence derived from a variety of techniques, including the computer simulation of a car accident (*Starr v. Campos,* 134 Ariz. 254, 655 P.2d 794 [1982]), hypnosis (*State ex rel. Collins v. Superior Court, Etc.,* 132 Ariz. 180, 644 P.2d 1266 [1982]), a multisystem method of blood analysis (*State v. Washington,* 229 Kan. 47, 622 P.2d 986 [1981]), hair analysis *(State v. Clawson,* 270 S.E.2d 659 (W. Va. App. Div. [1980]), and the polygraph (*State v. Dean,* 103 Wis.2d 228, 307 N.W.2d 628 [1981]), as well as two cases involving voice spectrography (*State v. Williams,* 4 Ohio St.3d 53, 446 N.E.2d 444 [1983]) and *Cornett v. State,* 450 N.E.2d 498 [Ind. 1983]). Note that *Shepard's* does not provide the full citation. You can obtain it, however, by starting with the citation that it does provide. Despite the obvious benefits of *Shepardizing,* the percentage of cases that are directly relevant to the specific topic of interest to the researcher or practitioner may be quite low.

Although citations obtained from the initial case, the digests, and *Shepard's* may result in some overlap, they are different enough from one another that reviewing them should be considered as complementary rather than alternative research techniques. Even with the overlap, however, it is not unusual for these methods to turn up hundreds of case citations—more than any beginning legal researcher can handle. Given the extensive amount of information to be absorbed, it would be advisable to start by reading a treatise, legal encyclopedia, or a few relevant law review articles to get a conceptual hook on how to order and evaluate this information.

The final step when searching for additional cases is to check the loose-leaf services and the advance sheets for recent cases on your topic from the sources described in the first part of this chapter.

Exercises

A. As a first exercise, find the volumes of *Maryland Reports, Atlantic Reporter,* and *American Law Reporter* that contain the *Reed* opinion and compare the information provided by these various reporters.

STATE

B. Given one citation, find the alternative citations(s) for the case and the name of the case.
   1. 249 A.2d 180
   2. 129 Vt. 583
   3. 301 A.2d 582
   4. 48 A.L.R.2d 1185
   5. 255 Ark. 517
   6. 349 S.W.2d 717
   7. 213 Neb. 686
   8. 97 N.M. 682
   9. 329 N.W.2d 386
   10. 53 Ohio St. 2d 123

C. Given the state and year in which the case was decided, as well as the squib that accompanies the case name and citation in the appropriate digest, find the case name and its citation.
   1. "Assault committed when hotel porter verbally abused paying hotel guests and struck guest in the face with fist after guest complained with regard to fact that porter dropped vacuum cleaner on guest's knee was not within scope of porter's employment and was not chargeable to employer under doctrine of respondeat superior." New York, 1976.
   2. "Evidence established that the fault of hospital employees who were responsible for counting of sponges during surgery was the sole cause of leaving of sponge in abdomen of patient suing both hospital and physician." Louisiana, 1968.

AUTHOR'S NOTE: The answers to these exercises follow at the end of this section.

3. "A search is a search and cannot be anything different simply because police officer conducting same chooses to characterize it as an inventory." New Jersey, 1973.
4. "A television set is not obvious contraband and there is nothing intrinsically wrong with walking down the street carrying one." D.C., 1978. (Hint: Try "Searches and Seizures.")
5. "A 'trick' is a professional engagement of a prostitute." Hawaii, 1963.
6. "Evidence established that undertaker's request that $17 which decedent's mother had agreed in writing to pay for tie, gloves, and conducting wake be paid before such merchandise was delivered along with body and casket and before wake was conducted was not an unreasonable or oppressive requirement such as would justify award of exemplary or punitive damages." Mississippi, 1953.
7. "Slaves, though generally immovable by law, are movable by nature." Louisiana, 1851. (Hint: Try "Property.")
8. "Where spider which had bitten plaintiff's decedent was not in bananas which were delivered by defendant grocers' organization but was on piece of wet burlap on top of box of radishes, under the bananas, neither doctrine of strict liability nor breach of implied warranty of fitness applied." Washington, 1974.
9. "Requirement that woman visitor to all-male prison wear a brassiere did not deny or abridge equality of rights under the law in violation of equal rights amendment of State Constitution." Hawaii, 1978.
10. "Although owner of cow was subject to liability in tort for damage he caused by improperly allowing cow to be at large, such liability did not affect his right to recover no-fault insurance benefits for damage caused to his cow when struck by truck on highway." Michigan, 1981.

D. For these questions, use *Shepard's* to assist you.
1. Has *Falk v. Finkelman,* 268 Mass. 524, 168 N.E. 89 (1929), ever been expressly followed in a subsequent case?
2. What happened to *Shaw v. Allied Finance Company,* 330 S.W.2d 690 (Tex. Civ. App. 1959), on appeal? What item of property caused the dispute?
3. Is *Hill v. St. Louis Public Service Co.,* 359 Mo. 220, 221 S.W.2d 130 (1949), still a good precedent?
4. Is *Frenel v. Commonwealth,* 331 S.W.2d 710 (Ky. 1959), still a good precedent? What was this case about?

FEDERAL

E. Given one citation, find the alternative citation(s) for the case, if any, and the name of the case.
   1. 40 L.Ed.2d 496
   2. 12 S.Ct. 892
   3. 364 U.S. 40
   4. 24 L.Ed.2d 299
   5. 57 S.Ct. 835
   6. 147 F.2d 749
   7. 153 U.S. App. D.C. 384
   8. 259 F.2d 65
   9. 505 F.2d 301
   10. 194 F.Supp. 297

F. Given the year in which the case was decided, as well as the squib that accompanies the case name and citation in the appropriate digest, find the case name and its citation.
   1. "Taxpayers may order their affairs so as to minimize taxes, since nobody owes any public duty to pay more than the law demands and taxes are enforced exactions, not voluntary contributions." 1947
   2. "Where it could not be determined how long a banana may have been on floor in defendant's supermarket before plaintiff stepped on it, fell and was injured, plaintiff was not entitled to recover from supermarket for injuries." 1968
   3. "Complaint alleging that union caused airline employer to permit male flight cabin attendants to marry while denying the same privilege to female attendants states a claim under Civil Rights Act of 2964 upon which relief could be granted." 1970
   4. "Where plaintiffs, owners of one-half interest in stallion, had been adjudicated in previous action to have no possessory right to stallion, and following the adjudication renounced right to possession by entering into management contract with defendants, recognition of defendants' right to possession would not be denied merely because plaintiffs instituted action for partition of the stallion." 1972
   5. "Question whether film *Last Tango in Paris* was obscene under the 1973 United States Supreme Court decision was a question for the trier of fact and could not be determined as a matter of law." 1973

6. "Criminal trespass convictions of Negroes who sat at lunch counter of drugstore, which had policy of permitting only white persons to sit and eat, and waited for service and who did nothing disorderly or anything other than politely ask for service would be reversed." 1964
7. "Decedent who was walking through wooded area when he saw blackened electric lines which were sagging eight to ten feet from ground and leapt up and grabbed both of the uninsulated lines, one in each hand, and was electrocuted was contributorily negligent as a matter of law." 1968
8. "The settling of fluorides upon gladiolus growers' property from aluminum reduction plant constituted trespass as a matter of law entitling growers to nominal damages as a matter of law." 1963
9. "There was no 'tacit agreement' in 1947 Paris Peace Treaty that United States would retain custody of Hungarian coronation regalia until such time as Soviet troops were withdrawn from Hungary." 1977
10. "It is a matter of common knowledge that it is almost impossible for a man of ordinary means to support two major vices at the same time." 1975 (Hint: Try "Evidence.")

G. For these final questions, use *Shepard's* to assist you.
1. Briefly, with which substantive areas of law was the court concerned in *Lisner v. Chicago Title & Trust Co.,* 439 F.Supp. 1242 (S.D. Ill. 1977)? What was the disposition of these issues on appeal?
2. The question of whether a longshoreman suing to recover damages from a shipowner for injuries that he received while working on the ship could take his question to the jury was decided in the affirmative by the 2d Circuit Court of Appeals in *Lubrano v. Royal Netherlands Steamship Co.,* 572 F.2d 364 (1978). Did this affirm or reverse the trial court's holding?
3. According to *Hackley v. Roudebush,* 520 F.2d 108 (D.C. Cir. 1975), is a federal employee entitled to a trial de novo when he or she is dissatisfied with the administrative proceedings concerning his or her discrimination claim? How had the lower court in this case decided the issue?
4. Trace the subsequent history of *Green v. Santa Fe Industries, Inc.,* 391 F.Supp. 849 (S.D. N.Y. 1975).
5. The defendant in *United States v. Salvucci,* 599 F.2d 1094 (1st Cir. 1979), wanted to suppress certain evidence at trial about his unlawful possession of stolen checks, alleging that this information had been obtained through an illegal search and seizure. Did the Supreme Court agree with the circuit court's decision to suppress?

Answers to Exercises

STATE

A. Requires no written response.

B.
1. *Atlantic Gulf & Pac. Co. v. State Dep't of Assessments & Taxation,* 252 Md. 173 (1969).
2. *Wetmore v. Wetmore,* 285 A.2d 711 (1971).
3. *Commonwealth v. Pride,* 450 Pa. 557 (1973).
4. *Carpineta v. Shields,* 70 So.2d 573 (Fla. 1954).
5. *Thomas v. Committee "A" Arkansas State Plant Bd.,* 501 S.W.2d 248 (1973).
6. *Rudman v. R.R. Comm'n of Texas,* 162 Tex. 579 (1961).
7. *State v. Patterson,* 331 N.W.2d 500 (1983).
8. *State v. Beachum,* 643 P.2d 246 (1981).
9. *State v. Armstrong,* 110 Wis.2d 555 (1983).
10. *State v. Souel,* 372 N.E.2d 1318 (1978).

C.
1. *Moritz v. Pines Hotel, Inc.,* 52 A.D.2d 1020, 383 N.Y.S.2d 704 (1976). Topic is "Master and Servant."
2. *Grant v. Touro Infirmary,* 207 So.2d 235, affirmed in part, reversed in part, *Tyler v. Youro,* 254 La. 204, 223 So.2d 148 (1968). Topic is "Hospitals."
3. *State v. Jones,* 122 N.J.Super. 585, 301 A.2d 185 (1973). Topic is "Searches and Seizures."
4. *U.S. v. Pannell,* 383 A.2d 1078 (D.C. App. 1978). Topic is "Searches and Seizures."
5. *State v. Cavness,* 46 Haw. 470, 381 P.2d 685 (1963). Topic is "Prostitution."
6. *Arnold v. Spears,* 217 Miss. 209, 63 So.2d 850 (1953). Topic is "Dead Bodies."
7. *Hyams v. Smith,* 6 La.Ann. 362 (1851). Topic is "Property."
8. *Anderson v. Associated Grocers, Inc.,* 11 Wash.App. 774, 525 P.2d 284 (1974). Topic is "Products Liability."

9. *Holdman v. Olim,* 59 Haw. 346, 581 P.2d 1164 (1978). Topic is "Prisons."
10. *Citizens Ins. Co. of America v. Tuttle,* 411 Mich. 536, 309 N.W.2d 174 (1981). Topic is "Insurance."

D.
1. It was expressly followed in *Monteiga v. Farnham,* 5 Mass. App. 888, 369 N.E.2d 728 (1977).
2. The Texas Supreme Court reversed the case, 337 S.W.2d 107 (Tex. 1960). The dispute concerned a Cadillac automobile.
3. No, it was overruled in *Williams v. St. Louis Public Service Co.,* 363 Mo. 625, 253 S.W.2d 97 (1952).
4. No, it was overruled in *Commonwealth, Department of Highways v. Sherrod,* 367 S.W.2d 844 (Ky. 1963). It concerned the value of property subject to a condemnation proceeding.

FEDERAL

E.
1. *Bob Jones University v. Simon,* 416 U.S. 725, 94 S.Ct. 2038 (1974).
2. *McDonald v. Belding,* 145 U.S. 492, 36 L.Ed. 788 (1892).
3. *Armstrong v. United States,* 80 S.Ct. 1563, 4 L.Ed.2d 1554 (1960).
4. *Morales v. New York,* 396 U.S. 102, 90 S.Ct. 291 (1969).
5. *Duke v. United States,* 301 U.S. 492, 81 L.Ed. 1243 (1937).
6. *In re Ginsburg,* 2d Cir. 1945.
7. *United States v. Cooper,* 473 F.2d 95 (1972).
8. *Donovan v. Esso Shipping Company,* 3d Cir. 1958.
9. *United States v. Oliver,* 7th Cir. 1974.
10. *United States v. 3,276.21 Acres of Land, etc.,* S.D. Cal. 1961.

F.
1. *Atlantic Coast Line R. Co. v. Phillips,* 332 U.S. 168 (1947). Topic is "Taxation."
2. *Joye v. Great Atlantic & Pac. Tea Co.,* 405 F.2d 464 (4th Cir. 1968). Topic is "Negligence."
3. *Lansdale v. Air Line Pilots Ass'n Int'l.,* 430 F.2d 1341 (5th Cir. 1970). Topic is "Civil Rights."
4. *Gary v. Peckham,* 468 F.2d 1241 (10th Cir. 1972). Topic is "Partition."
5. *United Artists Corp. v. Harris,* 363 F.Supp. 857 (D. Okla. 1973). Topic is "Obscenity."

6. *Barr v. City of Columbia,* 378 U.S. 146 (1964). Topic is "Trespass."
7. *Thompson v. Pennsylvania Power Co.,* 402 F.2d 88 (3d Cir. 1968). Topic is "Electricity."
8. *Reynolds Metals Co. v. Lampert,* 316 F.2d 272 (9th Cir. 1963), reh'g 324 F.2d 465 (9th Cir. 1963), cert. denied 376 U.S. 910, 84 S.Ct. 664, 11 L.Ed.2d 608 (1964). Topic is "Trespass."
9. *Dole v. Carter,* 444 F.Supp. 1065 (D. Kan. 1977), motion denied 569 F.2d 1109 (10th Cir. 1977). Topic is "Treaties."
10. *U.S. v. Houghton,* 388 F.Supp. 773 (D. Tex. 1975). Topic is "Evidence."

G.
1. The trial court was dealing with issues involving the construction of a will, particularly the disposition of the decedent's real property. The 7th Circuit Court of Appeals reversed the trial court's decision and remanded the case for further consideration (582 F.2d 1092, 1978). The Supreme Court denied certiorari, 440 U.S. 961, 99 S.Ct. 1504, 59 L.Ed.2d 775 (1979).
2. The appellate court decision reversed the trial court's decision that had directed the verdict in favor of the shipowner.
3. Yes, he or she is entitled to a trial de novo. This reverses the lower court's holding, *Hackley v. Johnson,* 360 F.Supp. 1247 (D. D.C. 1973).
4. The Second Circuit Court of Appeals affirmed the trial court's decision in part and reversed it in part, 533 F.2d 1309 (1976). The Supreme Court reversed the circuit court's decision and remanded the case, 430 U.S. 462, 97 S.Ct. 1292, 51 L.Ed.2d 480 (1977). The Second Circuit reconsidered the issues and remanded the case to the original trial court at 567 F.2d 4 (1977). The trial court's final decision is found at 82 F.R.D. 688 (S.D. N.Y. 1979).
5. No, the Supreme Court reversed the circuit court's decision to suppress the evidence, 448 U.S. 83, 100 S.Ct. 2547, 65 L.Ed.2d 619 (1980).

Appendix 2.1

James Reed, Jr.

v.

State of Maryland

court's admission of voiceprint evidence. We hold that the admission of this evidence was error.[2]

The voiceprint technique, although of relatively recent origin, has been much discussed and described in cases and legal commentaries.[3] The process involves the use of a machine known as a spectrograph. This machine analyzes the acoustic energy of the human voice into three components—time, frequency, and intensity—and graphically displays these components by generating, through an electric stylus, a series of closely spaced light and dark lines, varying in position, on a sheet of electrically sensitive paper. The resulting graphic representation is what is called a spectrogram or "voiceprint." It reveals certain patterns or "formats" which correspond to the sounds which are analyzed. According to the testimony of Dr. Oscar Tosi, the State's principal witness at the suppression hearing and the most widely known proponent of the reliability of the voiceprint technique,[4] spectrography

"consists of comparing both aurally and visually spectrograms of a questioned voice and a known voice, and on the basis of the similarities to decide whether or not the two voices, the questioned and known voice are the same or belong to different persons."

Essentially, therefore, the task of spectrography is one of pattern matching. It is dependent on the individual judgment of the examiner. As stated by Dr. Tosi:

"I consider [spectrography] reliable only if the examiner is reliable and he adjusts to what the conditions are, and he is an honest person; and he is prone to use no opinion, but probability rather than positive identification in cases of some doubt. Then I consider this good. It is reliable and can be used only . . . under these circumstances. Otherwise it would be a disaster."

The examiner's task is complicated by what is termed "intra-speaker" variability, that is, the fact that individual speakers apparently do not say the same word in precisely the same way each time they utter it, and that spectrograms reflect this difference. According to Detective Sergeant Lonnie Smrkovski of the Michigan State Police, the examiner in the instant case, if a speaker were to utter the same word on fifty consecutive days, he would expect none of the resulting spectrograms to be

2. Our grant of certiorari also encompassed Reed's alternate argument that the Best Evidence Rule was violated when the trial court permitted either a second or a third-hand copy of the tapes of the September 1974 calls to be used for comparison with Reed's voice exemplars. Reed maintains that the original tapes were destroyed through gross negligence of the investigating police officers, and that the second copy was lost or destroyed without explanation. However, in light of our ruling on Reed's principal claim, it is unnecessary for us to reach this alternate issue.

3. See, e. g., United States v. Baller, 519 F.2d 463 (4th Cir. 1975), cert. denied, 423 U.S. 1019, 96 S.Ct. 456, 46 L.Ed.2d 391 (1975); United States v. Franks, 511 F.2d 25 (6th Cir. 1975), cert. denied, 422 U.S. 1042, 95 S.Ct. 2654, 45 L.Ed.2d 693 (1975); United States v. Addison, 162 U.S.App.D.C. 199, 498 F.2d 741 (1974); People v. Kelly, 17 Cal.3d 24, 130 Cal.Rptr. 144, 549 P.2d 1240 (1976); Commonwealth v. Lykus, 367 Mass. 191, 327 N.E.2d 671 (1975); State ex rel. Trimble v. Hedman, 291 Minn. 442, 192 N.W.2d 432 (1971); Commonwealth v. Topa, 471 Pa. 223, 369 A.2d 1277 (1977). See also Comment, The Voiceprint Dilemma: Should Voices Be Seen and Not Heard?, 35 Md.L.Rev. 267 (1975); Decker and Handler, Voiceprint Identification Evidence—Out of the Frye Pan and into Admissibility, 26 Am.U.L. Rev. 314 (1977); Greene, Voiceprint Identification: The Case in Favor of Admissibility, 13 Am.Crim.L.Rev. 171 (1975); Jones, Danger— Voiceprints Ahead, 11 Am.Crim.L.Rev. 549 (1973); Jones, Evidence Vel Non The Non Sense of Voiceprint Identification, 62 Ky.L.J. 301 (1974); Kamine, The Voiceprint Technique: Its Structure and Reliability, 6 San Diego L.Rev. 213 (1969); Hollien and McGlone, The Effect of Disguise on "Voiceprint" Identification, 2 J. of Crim.Def. 117 (1976).

4. Dr. Tosi is Professor of Audiology and Speech Sciences and Physics at Michigan State University. He holds two Ph.D.'s, one in Audiology and Speech Sciences from Ohio State University, the other in Engineering and Physics from Buenos Aires University. He is a member of various professional societies and has published several books and numerous papers.

REED v. STATE
Cite as 391 A.2d 364

identical.[5] It is maintained, however, that the differences between the separate utterances of an individual speaker are less than the differences between the utterances of different speakers, so that intra-speaker variations do not render identification impossible.

According to Sgt. Smrkovski, at least ten points of similarity must be noted between two speech samples before a positive identification can be achieved. Apparently, this is independent of the number of the speech samples being compared. In the instant case, Sgt. Smrkovski, after listening to the tapes submitted to him, selected 138 of the 2,162 words spoken for comparison and made spectrograms of these words. In this sample, Sgt. Smrkovski rated one comparison "excellent," twenty "very good," thirty-seven "good," and thirty-five "fair." These comparisons were the basis of his conclusion that Reed's voice and the voice of the victim's caller were the same.

A principal consideration with regard to the admissibility of expert testimony, according to Wigmore, is: "On *this subject* can a jury receive from *this person* appreciable help?" 7 Wigmore, *Evidence* § 1923 (Chadbourn rev. 1978). Clearly, this is dependent on the particular circumstances of each case. No rule or set of rules could be expressed for all cases which would adequately distinguish helpful expert testimony from that which is superfluous or worse. Accordingly, this Court has held that the determination of similar and related issues are generally matters within the sound discretion of the trial court. *Beahm v. Shortall,* 279 Md. 321, 340, 368 A.2d 1005 (1977); *Greenstein v. Meister,* 279 Md. 275, 283, 368 A.2d 451 (1977); *Radman v. Harold,* 279 Md. 167, 168, 367 A.2d 472 (1977), and cases there cited.

On the other hand, with particular regard to expert testimony based on the application of new scientific techniques, it is recognized that prior to the admission of such testimony, it must be established that the particular scientific method is itself reliable. *People v. Kelly,* 17 Cal.3d 24, 130 Cal.Rptr. 144, 549 P.2d 1240 (1976); Jones, *Danger—Voiceprints Ahead,* 11 Am.Crim.L.Rev. 549, 554 (1973). See also *Shanks v. State,* 185 Md. 437, 440, 45 A.2d 85 (1945); 3 Wigmore, *Evidence* § 795 (Chadbourn rev. 1970).

[1] On occasion, the validity and reliability of a scientific technique may be so broadly and generally accepted in the scientific community that a trial court may take judicial notice of its reliability. Such is commonly the case today with regard to ballistics tests, fingerprint identification, blood tests, and the like. See *Shanks v. State, supra,* 185 Md. at 440, 45 A.2d 85. Similarly, a trial court might take judicial notice of the invalidity or unreliability of procedures widely recognized in the scientific community as bogus or experimental. However, if the reliability of a particular technique cannot be judicially noticed, it is necessary that the reliability be demonstrated before testimony based on the technique can be introduced into evidence. Although this demonstration will normally include testimony by witnesses, a court can and should also take notice of law journal articles, articles from reliable sources that appear in scientific journals, and other publications which bear on the degree of acceptance by recognized experts that a particular process has achieved. *People v. Law,* 40 Cal.App.3d 69, 75, 114 Cal.Rptr. 708, 711 (1974).

The question of the reliability of a scientific technique or process is unlike the question, for example, of the helpfulness of particular expert testimony to the trier of facts in a specific case. The answer to the question about the reliability of a scientific technique or process does not vary according to the circumstances of each case. It is therefore inappropriate to view this threshold question of reliability as a matter within each trial judge's individual discretion. In-

---

5. Sergeant Smrkovski has been employed by the Michigan Department of State Police for ten years, the last four and one-half as officer in charge of the voice identification unit. At the time of the hearing, he was about to receive his bachelor's degree in audiology and speech science from Michigan State University.

stead, considerations of uniformity and consistency of decision-making require that a legal standard or test be articulated by which the reliability of a process may be established.

The test which has gained general acceptance throughout the United States for establishing the reliability of such scientific methods was first articulated in the leading case of *Frye v. United States*, 54 U.S.App. D.C. 46, 47, 293 F. 1013, 1014 (1923):

> "Just when a scientific principle or discovery crosses the line between the experimental and demonstrable stages is difficult to define. Somewhere in this twilight zone the evidential force of the principle must be recognized, and while courts will go a long way in admitting expert testimony deduced from a *well-recognized* scientific principle or discovery, the thing from which the deduction is made must be *sufficiently established to have gained general acceptance in the particular field in which it belongs.*" (Emphasis supplied.)

That is to say, before a scientific opinion will be received as evidence at trial, the basis of that opinion must be shown to be generally accepted as reliable within the expert's particular scientific field. Thus, according to the *Frye* standard, if a new scientific technique's validity is in controversy in the relevant scientific community, or if it is generally regarded as an experimental technique, then expert testimony based upon its validity cannot be admitted into evidence.

The identity of the relevant scientific community is, of course, a matter which depends upon the particular technique in question. In general, members of the relevant scientific community will include those whose scientific background and training are sufficient to allow them to comprehend and understand the process and form a judgment about it. In unusual circumstances, a few courts have held that the experts thus qualified might properly be from a somewhat narrower field. See *People v. Williams*, 164 Cal.App.2d Supp. 858, 331 P.2d 251 (1958).

This criterion of "general acceptance" in the scientific community has come to be the standard in almost all of the courts in the country which have considered the question of the admissibility of scientific evidence. See, e. g., *Rivers v. Black*, 259 Ala. 528, 68 So.2d 2 (1953); *Pulakis v. State*, 476 P.2d 474 (Alaska 1970); *State v. Valdez*, 91 Ariz. 274, 371 P.2d 894 (1962); *People v. Busch*, 56 Cal.2d 868, 16 Cal.Rptr. 898, 366 P.2d 314 (1961); *People v. Williams*, supra; *Brooke v. People*, 139 Colo. 388, 339 P.2d 993 (1959); *Kaminski v. State*, 63 So.2d 339 (Fla. 1953); *Salisbury v. State*, 221 Ga. 718, 146 S.E.2d 776 (1966); *State v. Linn*, 93 Idaho 430, 462 P.2d 729 (1969); *State v. Lowry*, 163 Kan. 622, 185 P.2d 147 (1947); *State v. Casale*, 150 Me. 310, 110 A.2d 588 (1954); *Commonwealth v. Fatalo*, 346 Mass. 266, 191 N.E.2d 479 (1963); *People v. Morse*, 325 Mich. 270, 38 N.W.2d 322 (1949); *State v. Kolander*, 236 Minn. 209, 52 N.W.2d 458 (1952); *State v. Stout*, 478 S.W.2d 368 (Mo. 1972); *Boeche v. State*, 151 Neb. 368, 37 N.W.2d 593 (1949); *State v. Arnwine*, 67 N.J.Super. 483, 171 A.2d 124 (1961); *State v. Trimble*, 68 N.M. 406, 362 P.2d 788 (1961); *People v. Alston*, 79 Misc.2d 1077, 362 N.Y.S.2d 356 (1974); *State v. Steele*, 27 N.C.App. 496, 219 S.E.2d 540 (1975); *State v. Swanson*, 225 N.W.2d 283 (N.D. 1974); *State v. Smith*, 50 Ohio App.2d 183, 362 N.E.2d 1239 (1976); *Henderson v. State*, 94 Okl.Cr. 45, 230 P.2d 495 (1951); *State v. Green*, 271 Or. 153, 531 P.2d 245 (1975); *United States v. Bruno*, 333 F.Supp. 570 (E.D. Pa. 1971); *Romero v. State*, 493 S.W.2d 206 (Tex.Cr.App. 1973); *State v. Woo*, 84 Wash.2d 472, 527 P.2d 271 (1974); *Puhl v. Milwaukee Automobile Ins. Co.*, 8 Wis.2d 343, 99 N.W.2d 163 (1959).[6]

---

6. See, in addition, Wigmore, *The Science of Judicial Proof* § 220, p. 450 (3d ed. 1937):

"But, since the additions thus made possible to our unaided senses are due to the use of instruments constructed on knowledge of scientific laws, it is plain that the correctness of the data thus obtainable must depend upon the correctness of the instrument in construction and the ability of the technical witness to use it. Hence, the following three fundamental propositions apply to testimony based on the use of all such instruments:

Although *Frye v. United States, supra*, was a case involving the results of a lie detector examination, the test itself has been broadly applied, and judged the appropriate standard to apply to newly developed methods of scientific discovery. The *Frye* test has been invoked by courts in their consideration of, *inter alia*, paraffin test, *Brooke v. People, supra*; medical testimony regarding the cause of birth defects, *Puhl v. Milwaukee Automobile Ins. Co., supra*; breath analysis devices designed to test for intoxication, *People v. Morse, supra*; truth serum injections, *State v. Linn, supra*; blood tests, *People v. Alston, supra*; neutron activation analysis, *State v. Stout, supra*; gunshot residue tests, *State v. Smith, supra*; Nalline tests for detection of narcotics use, *People v. Williams, supra*; ink identification tests, *United States v. Bruno, supra*; and hypnotism, *People v. Busch, supra*.

This Court in *Shanks v. State, supra*, although not citing the *Frye* case itself, recognized the standard of general scientific acceptance in connection with the admissibility of blood test evidence. Chief Judge Marbury there pointed out (185 Md. at 440, 45 A.2d at 86, emphasis supplied):

"In the early cases evidence of the tests was not admitted, because the courts here were not convinced of their *general acceptance* and reliability. See *State v. Damm*, 62 S.D. 123, 252 N.W. 7; *Beuschel v. Manowitz*, 241 App.Div. 888, 272 N.Y.S. 165. Blood tests are *now accepted everywhere, scientifically, as accurate*, and the courts . . . have generally followed the same view."

Almost every state court that has considered voiceprint evidence in a reported opinion has applied the *Frye* or a similar standard in determining the question of its admissibility. See *Hodo v. Superior Court*, 30 Cal.App.3d 778, 784, 106 Cal.Rptr. 547, 550 (1973); *People v. Kelly*, 17 Cal.3d 24, 130 Cal.Rptr. 144, 549 P.2d 1240 (1976); *People v. Law, supra; People v. King*, 266 Cal.App.2d 437, 72 Cal.Rptr. 478 (1968); *Brown v. United States*, 384 A.2d 647 (D.C. C.A. 1978); *Worley v. State*, 263 So.2d 613, 614 (Fla.App. 1972); *Commonwealth v. Lykus*, 367 Mass. 191, 327 N.E.2d 671, 678 (1975); *People v. Tobey*, 401 Mich. 141, 257 N.W.2d 537 (1977); *State v. Cary*, 99 N.J. Super. 323, 239 A.2d 680, 685 (1968), *aff'd*, 56 N.J. 16, 264 A.2d 209 (1970); *D'Arc v. D'Arc*, 157 N.J.Super. 553, 385 A.2d 278 (1978); *People v. Rogers*, 86 Misc.2d 868, 385 N.Y.S.2d 228, 237 (1976); *State v. Olderman*, 44 Ohio App.2d 130, 336 N.E.2d 442, 448 (1975); *Commonwealth v. Topa*, 471 Pa. 223, 369 A.2d 1277, 1281 (1977). *Contra, State ex rel. Trimble v. Hedman*, 291 Minn. 442, 192 N.W.2d 432 (1971) (scientific disagreement goes to weight, not admissibility); *see also Alea v. State*, 265 So.2d 96 (Dist.Ct. App. Fla. 1972) (issue not discussed).

The *Frye* test has been subjected to some criticism, primarily on the grounds that it is too conservative and unduly prevents or delays the admission of relevant scientific evidence. *United States v. Sample*, 378 F.Supp. 44, 53 (E.D.Pa. 1974); McCormick, Evidence § 203, pp. 490–491 (2d ed. 1972); *cf. United States v. Baller*, 519 F.2d 463, 466 (4th Cir. 1975), *cert. denied*, 423 U.S. 1019, 96 S.Ct. 456, 46 L.Ed.2d 391 (1975). There are, however, compelling reasons which justify the *Frye* principle.

[2] Fairness to a litigant would seem to require that before the results of a *scientif-*

A. The type of apparatus purporting to be constructed on scientific principles must be accepted as dependable for the proposed purpose by the profession concerned in that branch of science or its related art. This can be evidenced by qualified expert testimony; or, if notorious, it will be judicially noticed by the judge without evidence.
B. The particular apparatus used by the witness must be one constructed according to an accepted type and must be in good condition for accurate work. This may be evidenced by a qualified expert.
C. The witness using the apparatus as the source of his testimony must be one qualified for its use by training and experience.

"These fundamentals will in the ordinary case be evidenced readily. But in every branch of science there are charlatans and incompetents. The recognition of the above fundamentals will usually serve to diminish the risk of unreliable testimony."

ic process can be used against him, he is entitled to a *scientific* judgment on the reliability of that process.[7] As stated by Judge McGowan, speaking for the court in *United States v. Addison,* 162 U.S.App.D.C. 199, 201, 498 F.2d 741, 743–744 (1974):

"[T]he *Frye* standard retards somewhat the admission of proof based on new methods of scientific investigation by requiring that they attain sufficient currency and status to gain the general acceptance of the relevant scientific community. This is not to say, however, that the *Frye* standard exacts an unwarranted cost. The requirement of general acceptance in the scientific community assures that those most qualified to assess the general validity of a scientific method will have the determinative voice."

This is an especially significant consideration with regard to those scientific techniques in which highly subjective judgments are based upon the data received from sophisticated mechanical devices. In these circumstances, the apparent objectivity of the machine may suggest a degree of certainty inconsistent with the subjective aspects of the enterprise.[8] *United States v. Addison, supra,* 162 U.S.App.D.C. at 202, 498 F.2d at 744; *People v. Kelly, supra.* As the Supreme Court of California stated in *Kelly* (130 Cal.Rptr. at 149, 549 P.2d at 1245):

". . . *Frye* was deliberately intended to interpose a substantial obstacle to the unrestrained admission of evidence based upon new scientific principles. . . Several reasons founded in logic and common sense support a posture of judicial caution in this area. Lay jurors tend to give considerable weight to 'scientific' evidence when presented by 'experts' with impressive credentials. We have acknowledged the existence of a '. . . misleading aura of certainty which often envelops a new scientific process, obscuring its currently experimental nature.' (*Huntingdon v. Crowley, supra,* 64 Cal.2d 647 at p. 656, 51 Cal.Rptr. 254 at p. 262, 414 P.2d 382 at p. 390; . . . .) As stated in *Addison, supra,* in the course of rejecting the admissibility of voiceprint testimony, 'scientific proof may in some instances assume a posture of mystic infallibility in the eyes of a jury . . . .' (*United States v. Addison, supra,* 498 F.2d at p. 744.)"

In addition to the advantage of substituting scientific for lay judgment as to scientific reliability, the court in *United States v. Addison, supra,* 162 U.S.App.D.C. at 202, 498 F.2d at 744, pointed out that the *Frye* test

". . . protects prosecution and defense alike by assuring that a minimal reserve of experts exists who can critically examine the validity of a scientific determination in a particular case. . . [T]he ability to produce rebuttal experts, equally conversant with the mechanics and methods of a particular technique, may prove to be essential."

The dissenting opinion, however, suggests that instead we adopt the rule enunciated by McCormick, that "[a]ny relevant conclusions which are supported by a qualified expert witness should be received unless there are other reasons for exclusion." *McCormick on Evidence* § 203 at 491 (2d ed. 1972). McCormick, in opposition to the great weight of judicial authority, believes

---

7. In 1665, in what may be one of the first reported instances of expert testimony, a certain Dr. Brown of Norwich, testifying at a trial, delivered of himself the expert scientific opinion that the accused were witches and, by practicing their witchcraft at the devil's bidding, had bewitched several children. The accused were found guilty and hanged. A Trial of Witches at Bury St. Edmonds, 6 Howell's State Trials 687, 697 (1665). No issue seems to have been raised in that case concerning the validity of the process for determining whether one was a witch.

8. *See, e. g.,* Highleyman, *The Deceptive Certainty of the "Lie Detector",* 10 Hastings L.J. 47, 63 (1958): "[T]he use of 'lie detector' evidence invites confusion between (1) the reliability of the objective physiological facts which are recorded by the polygraph, and (2) the reliability of the subjective inferences of truth or deception which are drawn from those facts by the examiner."

that disagreement in the scientific community regarding the reliability of a scientific process should go to the weight rather than the admissibility of scientific evidence.

[3] This view seems to us unacceptable. It fails to recognize that laymen should not on a case by case basis resolve a dispute in the scientific community concerning the validity of a new scientific technique. When the positions of the contending factions are fixed in the scientific community, it is evident that controversies will be resolved only by further scientific analysis, studies and experiments. Juries and judges, however, cannot experiment. If a judge or jurors have no foundation, either in their experience or in the accepted principles of scientists, on which they might base an informed judgment, they will be left to follow their fancy.[9] Thus, courts should be properly reluctant to resolve the disputes of science. "It is not for the law to experiment but for science to do so," *State v. Cary, supra,* 99 N.J.Super. at 332, 239 A.2d at 684.

Nonetheless, under the McCormick standard, juries would be compelled to make determinations regarding the validity of experimental or novel scientific techniques. As a result, one jury might decide that a particular scientific process is reliable, while another jury might find that the identical process is not. However, the reliability of the underlying technique or process to perform as it is supposed to does not vary with different cases. Using the polygraph as an example, although particular polygraph tests may give different results under different circumstances, the basic validity of the polygraph technique in general to give the type of results which are claimed for it does not change with the facts of each case. Nevertheless, if the trier of facts is to determine the *validity* of the polygraph test on a case by case basis, one judge or jury might determine that it is reliable and convict or acquit a defendant on the basis of the test results, whereas the very next judge or jury, sitting in the same courthouse and listening to the same operator giving the same type of test results, might determine that the technique is unreliable and ignore the results. Such inconsistency concerning the validity of a given scientific technique or process would be intolerable. See *Commonwealth v. Sullivan,* 146 Mass. 142, 145, 15 N.E. 491 (1888) (Holmes, J.).

Under the *Frye* test, however, this difficulty is largely avoided. As long as the scientific community remains significantly divided, results of controversial techniques will not be admitted, and all defendants will face the same burdens. If, on the other hand, a novel scientific process does achieve general acceptance in the scientific community, there will likely be as little dispute over its reliability as there is now concerning other areas of forensic science which have been deemed admissible under the *Frye* standard, such as blood tests, ballistics tests, etc.

In addition, there is a related danger under the McCormick view. The introduction of evidence based on a scientific process, not yet generally accepted in the scientific community, is likely to distract the fact finder from its central concern, namely the rendition of a judgment on the merits of the litigation. Without the *Frye* test or something similar, the reliability of an experimental scientific technique is likely to become a central issue in each trial in which it is introduced, as long as there remains serious disagreement in the scientific community over its reliability. Again and again, the examination and cross-examination of expert witnesses will be as protracted and time-consuming as it was at the trial in the instant case, and proceedings may well degenerate into trials of the technique

---

9. *See* 2 Wigmore, *Evidence* § 659, p. 771 (1940):

"When the testimony, thus appearing to the ordinary layman to lack a rational basis, is founded on observations made with esoteric methods or apparatus—*vacuum-rays, telepathy,* and the like—this method should be explained by the witness; and, *if it is vouched for as accepted in his branch of learning,* it suffices to admit his testimony." (Emphasis supplied.)

itself.[10] The *Frye* test is designed to forestall this difficulty as well. As stated in *State v. Cary, supra*, 99 N.J.Super. at 332, 239 A.2d at 684:

"All scientific aids and devices go through an experimental and testing stage, and during these stages there may be considerable scientific controversy. During this period of controversy . . the danger is that a trial may actually result in the trial of the technique rather than the trial of the issues involved in the case, if some less exacting rule is substituted for the time-honored rule of general scientific acceptance, ..."

[4] For the foregoing reasons, we agree with the "general acceptance" rule which the *Frye* case sets forth.

[5] Our adoption of the *Frye* standard does not, of course, disturb the traditional discretion of the trial judge with respect to the admissibility of expert testimony. *Frye* sets forth only a legal standard which governs the trial judge's determination of a threshold issue. Cf. *Radman v. Harold, supra*, 279 Md. at 169, 367 A.2d 472. Testimony based on a technique which is found to have gained "general acceptance in the scientific community" may be admitted into evidence, but only if a trial judge also determines in the exercise of his discretion, as he must in all other instances of expert testimony, that the proposed testimony will be helpful to the jury, that the expert is properly qualified, etc. Obviously, however, if a technique does not meet the *Frye* standard, a trial judge will have no occasion to reach these further issues.

Turning to the admissibility of testimony based on the voiceprint process, prior to 1972 it was generally agreed that the voiceprint process had not been sufficiently tested and accepted to qualify its results for use in the courts.[11] The Technical Committee on Speech Communication of the Acoustical Society of America had requested six scientists in the field of acoustics to evaluate the voiceprint process. These scientists, Richard Bolt, Franklin Cooper, Edward David, Peter Denes, James Pickett and Kenneth Stevens, reported in 1970 that the voiceprint process was still in its experimental stage, and the reliability of the conclusions based on the data obtained from the process was uncertain (*Speaker Identification by Speech Spectrograms: A Scientists' View of Its Reliability for Legal Purposes*, 47 J. Acoustical Soc'y Am. 597, 603 (1970)):

"[T]he available results are inadequate to establish the reliability of voice identification by spectrograms. We believe this conclusion is shared by most scientists who are knowledgeable about speech; hence, many of them are deeply concerned about the use of spectrographic evidence in the courts."

In 1971 and 1972, Dr. Tosi and his associates published a series of papers concerning the results of an experiment conducted on the voiceprint process.[12] Subsequently, some courts, relying exclusively on the testimony of Dr. Tosi and his Michigan associates, admitted in evidence testimony based

---

10. See, e. g., the dissent's observations in *United States v. Wright*, 17 U.S.C.M.A. 183, 194, 37 C.M.R. 447 (1967):

    "The trial was virtually concerned with nothing else but the efficacy and infallibility of the voiceprint process. The court's questions were directed almost completely to its effectiveness and demonstrated the members' extreme interest in its identification of the accused, to the exclusion of all others. Moreover, the trial counsel made the process the focal point of his argument, devoting approximately sixty percent thereof to its reliability."

11. See *State v. Cary*, 56 N.J. 16, 264 A.2d 209 (1970); *People v. King*, 266 Cal.App.2d 437, 72 Cal.Rptr. 478 (1968). *But see United States v. Wright*, 17 U.S.C.M.A. 183 (1967).

12. O. Tosi, H. Oyer, W. Lashbrook, C. Pedrey, and J. Nicol, *Voice Identification through Acoustic Spectrography*, Speech and Hearing Sci. Lab., Michigan State Univ., Rep. No. 171 (1971); O. Tosi, H. Oyer, W. Lashbrook, C. Pedrey, J. Nicol, and E. Nash, *An Experiment on Voice Identification: Excerpts from Report SHSLR 171*, Dep't of Audiology and Speech Sciences, Michigan State University, East Lansing, Michigan (July 1971); O. Tosi, H. Oyer, W. Lashbrook, C. Pedrey, J. Nicol, and E. Nash, *Experiment on Voice Identification*, 51 J. Acoustical Soc'y of Am. 2030 (1972).

on the voiceprint process. *See State ex rel. Trimble v. Hedman,* 291 Minn. 442, 192 N.W.2d 432 (1971); *Worley v. State,* 263 So.2d 613 (Dist.Ct.App. Fla. 1972) (use for corroboration); *Alea v. State,* 265 So.2d 96 (Dist.Ct.App. Fla. 1972) (following *Worley*); *Hodo v. Superior Court,* 30 Cal.App.3d 778, 106 Cal.Rptr. 547 (1973). However, as observed by Judge Kaplan, dissenting in *Commonwealth v. Lykus,* 367 Mass. 191, 327 N.E.2d 671, 680 (1975):

"It can fairly be said, however, that when the cases were decided the scientific community had not had sufficient time to study Dr. Tosi's work and reach conclusions as to its possible advance over the previous work in the field. *See People v. Law,* 40 Cal.App.3d 69, 81–82, 114 Cal. Rptr. 708 (1974). The decisions thus reflected less a consensus in the relevant scientific community that the Tosi method was acceptable, than an absence of study on which an informed opinion could be based one way or the other."

In 1973, Bolt, Cooper, David, Denes, Pickett and Stevens again addressed the voiceprint issue, in light of the Tosi experiment.[13] The authors expressed their concern about certain aspects of the Tosi experiment. They mentioned the Tosi experiment's failure to consider the problems of mimicking or disguising of voices, changes in voice levels, and changes due to stress or other emotional states of the speaker. They expressed further concern over the increase in error rates in comparing voice samples taken at different times, as well as the increase of error in other circumstances. The authors concluded, Bolt, et al., *Speaker Identification by Speech Spectrograms: Some Further Observations,* 54 J. Acoustical Soc'y Am. 531, 533–534 (1973):

"The Tosi study has improved our understanding of some of the problems of voice identification from spectrograms by indicating the influence of several important variables on the accuracy of identification. In uncovering factors that tend to increase identification errors, however, the study has not given us a definitive answer to the question: 'How reliably can a person be identified by examining the spectrographic patterns of his speech sounds?' Under certain laboratory conditions and for some selected sample of the population, the probability of making an error in identification can be stated. But for the less-than-ideal conditions encountered in forensic situations, the indications are that the probability of error will increase substantially. Further studies are needed, with particular attention to the examiner's decision criteria, the selection of speaker population, the time lapse between voice samples, background-noise conditions, and the psychological condition of the speaker.

"As scientists rather than lawyers, we offer no judgment as to whether or to what extent speech spectrograms should be used for identification in the courts. We wish only to point out that present methods for such use lack an adequate scientific basis for estimating reliability in many practical situations and that laboratory evaluations of these methods show increasing errors as the conditions for evaluation move toward real-life situations. We hope that our explanations of some of the factors that affect speaker identification will provide the legal profession with helpful information on which to base its own judgments concerning the admissibility of the spectrographic method."

The testimony in the instant case indicates that the fundamental division in the scientific community reflected in these articles has continued without substantial abatement. On direct examination of Dr. Tosi, he acknowledged the division in the scientific community concerning the validity of the voiceprint process:

"Q. How many experts within the field of sound spectrography that have used that process for voice identification oppose that process, who have done actual work in that field?

---

13. One of the authors, Kenneth Stevens, was apparently also a consultant in the Tosi experiment, Tosi, et al., *Experiment on Voice Identification, supra,* at 2043.

"A. In addition to the six authorities of Bolt, et al., and none of them worked in voice identification, Stevens had some nine years ago a small experiment. There are three others that oppose it that have done some work—not too much. Some of them have no professional basis. Let's say five of them, to the best of my knowledge.

"Q. How many of the experts within the field of sound spectrography for voice identification are in favor of that process?

"A. At least—I can give the names of at least 15, and among them very prominent scientists." [14]

Later, asked about the division of experts, excluding those professionally engaged in the field of voice identification, Tosi testified:

"A. Okay, five were opposed from this reduced group of persons that I said at least have published or done something but were not professionally engaged in the field. I say it is a rough number. Persons that I know of that have done some experimentation or have published, I said less than ten; five opposed—four or five are in favor. . . .

"Q. You are not including Dr. Bolt and his group, are you?

14. Tosi included in this group of supporters Dr. Peter Ladefoged. Ladefoged was originally an opponent of the voiceprint process (see Ladefoged and Vanderslice, The "Voiceprint" Mystique, 7 Working Papers in Phonetics 126 (1967)). Ladefoged testified in United States v. Raymond, 337 F.Supp. 641 (D.D.C. 1972), where voiceprint testimony was admitted. This result was overturned in United States v. Addison, 162 U.S.App.D.C. 199, 203, 498 F.2d 741, 745 (1974), where Judge McGowan, speaking for the court, observed that:

"[V]iewed in its entirety, Dr. Ladefoged's letter, as he himself characterized it . . . simply reflects a position 'of abatement of skepticism towards voiceprint,' not one of complete acceptance."

In addition, in Jones, Evidence Vel Non The Non Sense of Voiceprint Identification, 62 Ky. L.J. 301, 322 n. 96, Ladefoged is reported as responding to the question, "Would you say that 'voiceprints' as a method of voice identification now has general acceptance in the scientific community?" as follows:

"A. No, I am not."

Additional expert witnesses who testified for the State, in the instant case, were Sgt. Smrkovski, Dr. Peter Jansen and Dr. John A. McClung. Their testimony was consistent with that of Dr. Tosi in acknowledging the division in the scientific community.

Dr. Donald Baker, an expert witness called by the defense,[15] testified that spectrography was neither a reliable process nor generally accepted within the scientific community. Dr. Baker cited two samplings of opinion of the scientific community, both of which had been unfavorable toward the validity of the process. The first was a meeting in which the members of the Speech Communications Section of the Acoustical Society of America voted 42–0 against the efficacy of the procedure. The second was a mail survey, as reported in a scientific journal, which resulted in an unfavorable reaction. Dr. Baker also noted that the majority of articles on the subject were negative in their characterization of the process.

The extent of disagreement in the scientific community was emphasized in the instant case by the testimony of Dr. Henry Hollien,[16] another expert witness for the defense,[16] who stated:

"I think I did say that in some case; probably in the Washington case [i. e., United States v. Raymond] I said that. I think now I was in error to say that because, having said that, numerous of my friends, have said, 'No, not true.' I said it in good faith thinking that my friends had accepted it, and I now find that I have been reprimanded by some people."

15. Dr. Baker, who received his Ph.D. in Hearing and Speech Science from Ohio State University, is presently teaching graduate and undergraduate courses in hearing and speech at the University of Maryland. Dr. Baker testified that he had done research in related areas of spectrography and was familiar with the scientific literature concerning voice identification by spectrography.

16. Dr. Hollien holds advanced degrees including a Ph.D. from the University of Iowa. He is a professor of speech at the University of Florida and is director of the Institute for Advanced Study of Human Communication. He is the head of the Institute's research program on speaker identification. He is a member of vari-

"I have conducted or directed about six major studies using [the voiceprint] technique.

* * * * * *

"One of the things we have done, and we are the only people who have done this . . . we have applied our technique to . . . [simulated crimes], and it of course doesn't work.

* * * * * *

"There was nothing wrong with trying to use it [the technique]. It failed. Now it is an abuse.

"Q. It is an abuse because you feel there are some people not qualified to use it?

"A. No, no. It is the data. See, I don't think the people that use it know about the research literature. . . . There are many studies that have been published which show the problems with this. There is a huge literature that would demonstrate why they should back off, put a moratorium on this until we have some knowledge, and not foster this upon the judicial system and law enforcement agencies. *It amounts to a fraud.* I don't think they realize it. They don't know what is going on, you see." (Emphasis added.)

There has been a sharp division among the cases which have considered the admissibility of voiceprint evidence after the emergence of the controversy over Tosi's claims.

Three state supreme courts, California, Michigan and Pennsylvania, have held the evidence inadmissible. *Commonwealth v. Topa, supra; People v. Kelly, supra; People v. Tobey, supra.* In addition, the District of Columbia Court of Appeals, in *Brown v. United States,* 384 A.2d 647 (D.C. 1978), has also held voiceprint evidence inadmissible. On the other hand, the Supreme Court of Massachusetts has, in a divided opinion, held the evidence admissible, *Commonwealth v. Lykus, supra.* And see *State v. Williams,* 388 A.2d 500 (Me. 1978).

Two lower state courts have recently ruled voiceprint evidence admissible: *People v. Rogers,* 86 Misc.2d 868, 385 N.Y.S.2d 228 (1976); and *State v. Olderman,* 44 Ohio App.2d 130, 336 N.E.2d 442 (1975). However, in *D'Arc v. D'Arc,* 157 N.J.Super. 553, 385 A.2d 278 (1978), the New Jersey Superior Court ruled voiceprint evidence inadmissible.

In the United States Courts of Appeal, voiceprint evidence has been held inadmissible in *United States v. Addison, supra,* and admissible in *United States v. Baller, supra,* and *United States v. Franks,* 511 F.2d 25 (6th Cir. 1975), *cert. denied,* 422 U.S. 1042, 95 S.Ct. 2654, 45 L.Ed.2d 693 (1975).

All cases holding voiceprint evidence inadmissible have done so on the ground that the process fails to satisfy the standard articulated in *United States v. Frye, supra.* It is important to note, however, that neither *United States v. Baller, supra,* nor *United States v. Franks, supra,* in holding voiceprint evidence admissible, seemed to apply the *Frye* test. In *Franks,* the court stated (511 F.2d at 33):

"Although we, of course, *are aware of the differences of . . . scientific opinion concerning the use of voiceprints,* we also are mindful of 'a considerable area of discretion on the part of the trial judge in admitting or refusing to admit' evidence based on scientific processes." (Emphasis supplied.)

Similarly, in *United States v. Baller, supra,* the court, after considering the *Frye* standard, stated (519 F.2d at 466):

"Unless an exaggerated popular opinion of the accuracy of a particular technique makes its use prejudicial or likely to mislead the jury, it is better to admit relevant scientific evidence in the same manner as other expert testimony and allow its weight to be attacked by cross-examination and refutation."

The Massachusetts Supreme Court held that voiceprint analysis did satisfy the *Frye* standard. In *Commonwealth v. Lykus, supra,* 327 N.E.2d at 678 n. 6, that court stated:

---

ous societies, including the Academy for the Forensic Application of the Communications Sciences, of which he is a council member. He has authored over 100 major publications.

"[W]e agree that there certainly is not uniform and total acceptance of the [voiceprint] method [in the scientific community] . . . . Yet the . . . Frye standard does not require unanimity of view, only general acceptance; a degree of scientific divergence of view is inevitable. In this case we are disposed to give greater weight to those experts who have had direct and empirical experience in the field of spectrography. . .

"Thus, we find the evidence presented in support of the reliability of voiceprints, particularly as expressed in Dr. Tosi's study, sufficiently persuasive to outweigh the criticism expressed by certain other scientists in the field of acoustics."

Nevertheless, it is not fully clear whether the Massachusetts court was, consistent with the *Frye* standard, deciding that the voiceprint method is generally accepted by the scientific community or whether it was attempting itself to determine the merits of the claims of the various scientists. In any event, we find ourselves more in agreement with Judge Kaplan, dissenting in *Commonwealth v. Lykus, supra,* 327 N.E.2d at 682, who stated:

"To sum up, opinion is divided on the Tosi method; the journal material shows turbulence and discord rather than that 'general acceptance' which the *Frye* case lays down as a precondition of admissibility. Nor can it be plausibly said that those with adverse views are either unqualified to have opinions worthy of respect or are strangers to the relevant scientific 'field.' "

Furthermore, we disagree with the Massachusetts court's characterization of the nature of the dispute. A degree of scientific divergence of opinion is indeed inevitable, but the degree of divergence surrounding the voiceprint process is fundamental and goes to the very validity of the process itself. This kind and degree of divergence is notably absent in other areas of scientific evidence generally deemed admissible. As stated in Comment, *The Voiceprint Dilemma: Should Voices Be Seen and Not Heard?,* 35 Md.L.Rev. 267, 280 n. 79 (1975):

"[E]xperts may disagree as to the application of a technique, or as to the results of that application, *but they do not generally question that the technique is capable of producing the results claimed.* For instance, it is common knowledge that psychiatric diagnoses are often at odds with each other, and it is easy to picture experts disputing whether two writing samples came from the same hand. It is much more difficult to imagine experts disputing whether psychiatric diagnoses or handwriting identifications are possible with any significant degree of reliability. Yet that is precisely the nature of the voiceprint dispute; experts question the capability of the process itself, not just the results of its application." (Emphasis supplied.)

In addition, it is the almost unanimous opinion in recent legal commentaries that the voiceprint technique does not satisfy the standards articulated in *Frye v. United States. See, e. g.,* Comment, *The Voiceprint Dilemma: Should Voices Be Seen and Not Heard? supra* ; Comment, *Voiceprints: The End of the Yellow Brick Road,* 8 U.S.F. L.Rev. 702 (1974); Jones, *Danger—Voiceprints Ahead,* 11 Am.Crim.L.Rev. 549 (1973); Jones, *Evidence Vel Non The Non Sense of Voiceprint Identification,* 62 Ky. L.J. 301 (1974); Note, *Voiceprint Identification,* 61 Geo.L.J. 703 (1973); Thomas, *Voiceprint—Myth or Miracle (The Eyes Have It),* 3 U.San Fern.V.L.Rev. 15 (1974). Even those authors who advocate the admissibility of voiceprint evidence appear to concede that it does not meet the *Frye* test and argue instead for alternative revised standards under which it might be admissible. *See, e. g.,* Decker and Handler, *Voiceprint Identification Evidence—Out of the Frye Pan and into Admissibility,* 26 Am.U.L.Rev. 314, 361–365 (1977); Greene, *Voiceprint Identification: The Case in Favor of Admissibility,* 13 Am.Crim.L.Rev. 171, 195–197 (1975).

Despite this array, the trial court in the instant case determined that spectrography had achieved the standard of acceptance needed for admissibility. However, the trial court, in holding voiceprint evidence admissible, construed the *Frye* test to require "general acceptance . . . within the group actually engaged in the use of this technique and in the experimentation with this technique. . . . [W]e are restricting the relevant field of experts to those who are knowledgeable, directly knowledgeable through work, utilization of the techniques, experimentation and so forth, that we are not taking the broad general scientific community of speech and hearing science. In that broad community there probably is not acceptance."

We have serious doubts that voiceprint analysis meets even this reduced standard. Tosi's own testimony indicates substantial division of opinion among those who have done work or performed experiments relating to the voiceprint process.

In any event, we find that the trial court's formulation is inconsistent with the proper standard of acceptance necessary for admissibility. The circumstances of the instant case suggest no basis for "restricting the relevant field of experts" to those who have performed voiceprint experiments, and eliminating from consideration the opinions of those scientists in the fields of speech and hearing, as well as related fields, who, by training and education, are competent to make professional judgments concerning experiments undertaken by others. The purpose of the *Frye* test is defeated by an approach which allows a court to ignore the informed opinions of a substantial segment of the scientific community which stands in opposition to the process in question.

[6] Thus, based on our examination of the record in the instant case, the judicial opinions which have considered this question, and the available legal and scientific commentaries, we do not believe that "voiceprint" analysis has achieved the general acceptance in the scientific community, at this time, which is required under *Frye*. We therefore hold that testimony based on "voiceprints" or spectrograms is, for the present, inadmissible in Maryland courts as evidence of voice identification. This holding is, of course, subject to reconsideration by this Court if the use of spectrograms or some other technique of voice identification does in the future achieve the general acceptance of the scientific and legal communities.

JUDGMENT OF THE COURT OF SPECIAL APPEALS REVERSED, AND CASE REMANDED TO THAT COURT WITH DIRECTIONS TO REVERSE THE JUDGMENT OF THE CIRCUIT COURT FOR MONTGOMERY COUNTY AND REMAND THE CASE FOR A NEW TRIAL. MONTGOMERY COUNTY TO PAY COSTS.

SMITH, Judge.

I respectfully dissent. I believe the Court of Special Appeals was correct in holding that the expert might testify that in his opinion the voice of the person making the telephone calls in question was that of Reed. My dissent is based upon a number of reasons, not necessarily in the sequence in which I list them: (1) The rule enunciated in *Frye v. United States* (the *Frye* test), 54 App.D.C. 46, 293 F. 1013 (1923), is much criticized, has never been adopted in Maryland, and I am opposed to its adoption. (2) The decision here is out of step with that of a number of respected courts as to the basis for admission of evidence concerning expert opinions related to fingerprints, ballistics, X-ray, and the like. (3) The decision here is out of step with our prior Maryland holdings concerning expert testimony. (4) The majority of reported opinions which have considered the matter have permitted the admission of expert testimony relative to spectrographic analysis and voice identification. (5) Even if the *Frye* test were made applicable, the evidence here satisfied that test. I shall consider these points seriatim.

1. The *Frye* test

a. Views of authorities on the subject

Prior to the decision in *Reed v. State*, 35 Md.App. 472, 372 A.2d 243 (1977), *Frye* had never been cited in Maryland. Moreover, I fail to find where its concepts have previously been enunciated in Maryland. Obviously, it is in no way binding upon us.[1]

It should be noted at the outset that *Frye* was concerned with a type of situation materially different from that with which we are here faced. The defendant there was convicted of murder in the second degree. His sole assignment of error on appeal was the *refusal*[2] of the trial court to permit "an expert witness to testify to the result of a deception test made upon defendant." That test was a precursor of the present day polygraph, and was based solely on systolic blood pressure. The court said:

"[T]he theory seems to be that truth is spontaneous, and comes without conscious effort, while the utterance of a falsehood requires a conscious effort, which is reflected in the blood pressure. The rise thus produced is easily detected and distinguished from the rise produced by mere fear of the examination itself. In the former instance, the pressure rises higher than in the latter, and is more pronounced as the examination proceeds, while in the latter case, if the subject is telling the truth, the pressure registers highest at the beginning of the examination, and gradually diminishes as the examination proceeds." *Id.* at 1014.

Prior to the trial the defendant had been "subjected to this deception test, and counsel offered the scientist who conducted the test as an expert to testify to the results obtained." Apparently, it was intended to have the expert state that the defendant was telling the truth. It was in this context that the court said it thought "the systolic blood pressure deception test ha[d] not yet gained such standing and scientific recognition among physiological and psychological authorities as would justify the

---

1. I think Professor Wigmore is generally regarded as the outstanding authority, during his lifetime at least, in the field of evidence. I thus find it of interest that the only reference to *Frye* found in Wigmore, *Evidence* (3d ed. 1940), produced during Professor Wigmore's lifetime, is in a footnote to § 999 at p. 645 of Vol. 3. It states, "The use of the instrument (polygraph, cardiograph, pneumograph) when offered through expert testimony *on behalf of an accused*, has twice been rejected, in reported cases," referring to *Frye* and another case. (Emphasis in original.) The section is concerned with "Scientific Psychological Diagnosis of Testimony" and "the Blood-Pressure ('Lie-Detector') Method." The paragraph to which the footnote is appended states:

    "Thirdly, the fact of the lie might be used in *evidence at the trial*, as a basis for inference as to lies on other details of testimony— precisely as we infer from lies disclosed by the traditional method (*post*, § 1001). But this use of the machine-registered lie is rarely desirable and has not yet been judicially sanctioned by a Supreme Court." *Id.* at 645 (emphasis in original).

    To place the matter in context, the subtitle under which the above appears is "Testimonial Impeachment."

    Nowhere in this work, insofar as I can ascertain, does Professor Wigmore ever advocate a test relative to the admissibility of scientific evidence as rigid as that enunciated in *Frye* and adopted by the Court today.

    We are informed that the experiments which produced the techniques used in the case at bar began at Bell Telephone Laboratories during World War II. I find it of interest to note, however, that Professor Wigmore apparently foresaw such a technique, because in *The Science of Judicial Proof* § 156 (3d ed. 1937) he states:

    "*Vocal Traits.* By means of a well-understood principle, having many applications, the vibrations of the spoken voice on a diaphragm may be accurately translated, through an electrical current, into oscillations of a needle, and these oscillations may be arranged to leave a continuous variable ink-tracing as a record. It was long ago demonstrated that the vocal chords of a singer, in uttering the sustained notes of a song, have individuality, so that two such records of the same aria by different singers differ noticeably. Moreover the spoken voice, though its notes change their wave-lengths with far greater rapidity than the singing voice, can now also be made to leave a similar record having minute differences of individuality. The instrument available for this is a form of oscillograph. If now it can be proved that this individuality of the vocal organ (like the fingerprint) endures through a period of years, it is obvious that an additional mode of identification, readily recorded and classified, has become practicable." *Id.* at 284–85 (footnotes omitted).

    Note that for identification purposes Professor Wigmore was speaking in terms of comparisons of voice wave-lengths from records made years apart. No such lapse of time exists in the case at bar.

2. In other words, the appellate court merely affirmed the trial judge's exercise of discretion in excluding the evidence.

courts in admitting expert testimony deduced from the discovery, development, and experiments thus far made."

The evidence proposed in *Frye* was an obvious invasion of the province of the jury since the trier of fact is vested with the responsibility of determining the credibility of witnesses. It should be instantly perceived that the controversy here concerns a type of evidence vastly different from that rejected in *Frye*.

The *Frye* standard for determining admissibility of scientific evidence has been criticized by a number of respected scholars. Some object to the test generally. Others point to its inapplicability in the type of case at bar. Dean McCormick probably succeeded Professor Wigmore as the foremost authority in the field of evidence. *McCormick's Handbook of the Law of Evidence* § 203 at 489 (2d ed. 1972) states, "So far as it can be dated, the notion of a special rule of admissibility for scientific evidence seems to have arisen in 1923," referring to *Frye*. After pointing out that "[n]o authority was cited" for the court's conclusion in *Frye*, the authors state:

> " 'General scientific acceptance' is a proper condition for taking judicial notice of scientific facts, but not a criterion for the admissibility of scientific evidence. Any relevant conclusions which are supported by a qualified expert witness should be received unless there are other reasons for exclusion. Particularly, probative value may be overborne by the familiar dangers of prejudicing or misleading the jury, and undue consumption of time. If the courts used this approach, instead of repeating a supposed requirement of 'general acceptance' not elsewhere imposed, they would arrive at a practical way of utilizing the results of scientific advances." [3] *Id.* at 491 (footnotes omitted).

J. Richardson, *Modern Scientific Evidence* § 2.5 (2d ed. 1974) states:

"It has been urged that certain scientific tests, as the lie detector, should be barred because they are not infallible. Surely this represents a type of judicial prejudice, for infallibility has never been a test for the admissibility of evidence—scientific or otherwise. Universal acceptance can be ruled out for the same reason, and it is urged that general scientific acceptance is a proper condition for the court to take judicial notice of a scientific fact, without laying the usual foundation, but not a sound criterion for the admissibility of scientific evidence. Any relevant conclusions, which are supported by a qualified expert witness, in a field finding substantial scientific acceptance should be admitted in evidence, for its probative value to be weighed by competent fact-finders in the light of all the circumstances. The courts should not confuse novelty with want of acceptance in refusing to admit the results of scientific techniques which offer much in aiding to ascertain the truth." *Id.* at 24 (footnote omitted).

The same author in § 9.2 quotes *Frye* in a footnote and then states:

"Here the court lays down the test of *general acceptance*, which, though ill-defined, is too restrictive. Actually, the degree of scientific acceptance should go to probative value, not admissibility. Wigmore once wrote, 'All that should be required as a condition (to admissibility) is the preliminary testimony of a scientist that the proposed test is an accepted one in his profession and that it has a reasonable measure of precision in its indications.' Evidence, § 990 (2d ed. 1923)." *Id.* at 290 n. 8 (emphasis in original).

A statement by Professor Wigmore identical to that quoted by Professor Richardson is found in J. Wigmore, *Evidence* § 990 at 626 (3d ed. 1940). The reference in Wigmore is to psychological testing.

A. Moenssens, R. Moses & F. Inbau, *Scientific Evidence in Criminal Cases* § 12.06 at

---

[3]. C. McCormick, *Law of Evidence* § 170 at 363–64 (1954), contains a statement almost identical to that above quoted.

517 n. 9 (1973), in discussing voice identification by spectrograms, states, "It is debatable, of course, whether the 'general acceptance' test of *Frye* . . . which has for decades been used by courts in determining admissibility of novel scientific test results, is a proper prerequisite to admissibility." The authors then quote from McCormick, *Evidence* § 170 (1954), to the effect that general scientific acceptance "is a proper condition upon the court's taking judicial notice of scientific fact, but not a criterion for the admissibility of scientific evidence."

Professor Strong of the University of Oregon said in *Questions Affecting the Admissibility of Scientific Evidence*, 1970 U.Ill. L.F. 1 (1970):

"In addition to the requirement that the expert tendered be qualified to supply or apply the scientific principle or principles, there exists another requirement under which the testimony of persons professing acquaintance with principles unknown to the tribunal may be rejected. This requirement, which was first announced in *Frye v. United States*, is that the principle upon which the expert proposes to testify must have achieved general acceptance in the scientific community. However, unanimity of approval, manifestly impossible in a world still believed by some to be flat, is not required. The resulting standard, something greater than acceptance by the expert himself but less than acceptance by all experts in the field, is obviously somewhat lacking in definiteness. Some courts have seemingly rejected the *Frye* standard, and others have tailored it to fit unusual situations. Nevertheless, the rule continues to be widely accepted.

"In addition to the difficulties apparent in ascertaining whether a general proposition of science has or has not been generally accepted, the *Frye* standard has been criticized as overly rigorous and as introducing an element of inconsistency into the law of evidence." *Id.* at 10–11 (footnotes omitted).

Additional criticism of the *Frye* test is found in Decker & Handler, *Voiceprint Identification Evidence—Out of the Frye Pan and Into Admissibility*, 26 Am.U.L.Rev. 314 (1977). Specifically, it is stated:

"The judicial trend denying admissibility of voiceprint identification evidence was based on a literal interpretation of the *Frye* standard of general scientific acceptance. Since the standard was drawn from dicta and formulated more than fifty years prior to advancements in science and technology such as spectrographic identification analysis, it is necessary that its validity be re-examined.

"The standard enunciated in *Frye* is one that is 'neither common to criminal litigation nor easily applied in the individual case.' Since its inception, the *Frye* standard has been the subject of criticism because of the limiting effect it has had on judicial acceptance of new methods of scientific investigation. In light of the rationale behind the *Frye* rule and its practical application to voiceprint identification evidence cases, it is apparent that the criticism is quite warranted.

"One of the reasons for the rule was to prevent the development of arbitrary decisions on issues of admissibility. Yet, enunciation of the *Frye* standard, without any definitive criteria as to who and how large the pertinent scientific community must be, has unnecessarily limited the discretion a trial court should have in utilizing relevant input. Indeed, while the *Frye* standard was utilized in *State v. Cary* and *People v. King*, it was not until *United States v. Addison* that one could find a comprehensive discussion of general scientific acceptance and how it ought to operate in the spectrographic analysis setting." *Id.* at 361–62 (footnotes omitted).

The authors further comment relative to *Frye*:

"Proponents of logical relevancy have criticized the *Frye* test, and suggested that there would be greater unanimity in the treatment of all forms of scientific evidence if the *Frye* rule were modified in conformance with the doctrine of logical relevance. That is, scientific evidence could be submitted to the jury upon a showing of reasonable reliability. Based on its determination of the accuracy and reliability of the evidence, the jury would decide the weight to be accorded it. Boyce, *Judicial Recognition of Scientific Evidence in Criminal Cases*, 8 Utah L.Rev. 313, 325–26 (1963–64); Note, *Evolving Methods of Scientific Proof*, 13 N.Y.L.F. 67[9], 681–85 (196[8])." *Id.* at 362 n.304.

Gorecki, *Comment: Evidentiary Use of the Voice Spectrograph in Criminal Proceedings*, 77 Mil.L.Rev. 167, 169 (1977), notes, "Criticism has been leveled at the rigidity of the *Frye* scientific standard both generally and with respect to its application to the voice spectrograph technique," citing, in addition to Professor Strong's article which we have heretofore quoted, Note, *The Voiceprint Technique: A Problem in Scientific Evidence*, 18 Wayne L.Rev. 1365, 1383 (1972), and Note, *Evolving Methods of Scientific Proof*, 13 N.Y.L.F. 679 (1968). Major Gorecki does not list the pages where the criticism is found in the latter publication, but they are 683, 684–85, 747 and 749.

It is suggested by Boyce, *Judicial Recognition of Scientific Evidence in Criminal Cases*, 8 Utah L.Rev. 313 (1963–64):

"There seems to be little reason why courts should not allow juries to hear both sides of the question of the reliability of a particular form of scientific evidence and decide what, if any, weight it should be accorded, upon, of course, a foundation which shows there is a reasonable possibility of reliability." *Id.* at 325–26.

Some are of the view that the new Federal Rules of Evidence 702 and 703, governing expert testimony, have adopted the McCormick standard of "assisting the trier of fact" rather than the *Frye* requirement of "general scientific acceptance." Romero, *The Admissibility of Scientific Evidence Under the New Mexico and Federal Rules of Evidence*, 6 N.M.L.Rev. 187, 197 (1976); Comment, *Expert Testimony and Voice Spectrogram Analysis*, 1975 Wash.U.L.Q. 775, 782 n.27 (1975); and Comment, *Evidence-Admission of Voiceprints Does Not Exceed the Discretion of the Trial Judge—United States v. Franks*, 511 F.2d 25 (1975), 44 Cinn.L.Rev. 616, 621 (1975). Without discussing *Frye*, J. Weinstein and M. Berger, *Weinstein's Evidence* (1976), states:

"Doubts about whether an expert's testimony will be useful should generally be resolved in favor of admissibility unless there are strong factors such as time or surprise favoring exclusions. The jury is intelligent enough, aided by counsel, to ignore what is unhelpful in its deliberations." *Id.* at 702–9.

New Federal Rule 901 provides in pertinent part:

"(a) General provision.—The requirement of authentication or identification as a condition precedent to admissibility is satisfied by evidence sufficient to support a finding that the matter in question is what its proponent claims.

"(b) Illustrations.—By way of illustration only, and not by way of limitation, the following are examples of authentication or identification conforming with the requirements of this rule:

* * * * * *

"(3) Comparison by trier or expert witness.—Comparison by the trier of fact or by expert witnesses with specimens which have been authenticated.

* * * * * *

"(5) Voice identification.—Identification of a voice, whether heard firsthand or through mechanical or electronic transmission or recording, by opinion based upon hearing the voice at any time under circumstances connecting it with the alleged speaker."

Weinstein and Berger, *supra*, comment:

"Rule 901(b)(5) provides for the identification of any voice by any person who can connect the voice with the alleged speaker by 'hearing' the voice. This language does not preclude testimony by an expert witness who has not 'heard' the voice but who has identified it by the voiceprint technique. Cf. Rule 901(b)(3), (4)." *Weinstein's Evidence* at 901–61.

I find disappointing the fact that the majority opinion does not address itself more directly to these issues. The appellant was of the view that it was a question of fact as to whether a given technique has general scientific acceptance, which makes a lot of sense to me. If it were a question of fact, then obviously the determination would be by the trial judge and the standard for review would be the clearly erroneous basis specified in Maryland Rules 886 and 1086.

From the majority opinion, I find myself somewhat puzzled as to what groups are to be considered in determining whether a process has general scientific acceptance and what knowledge, qualifications, and experience are required in order for one to offer an opinion on the subject. In the case at hand I would suppose that anyone with graduate training in the field of physics would be a member "of the relevant scientific community . . . whose scientific background and training [would be] sufficient to allow [him] to comprehend and understand the process and form a judgment about it," to use the majority's words. Are we to undertake some kind of poll to determine whether there is general acceptance—or that the technique would be generally accepted by all of those so trained if they were informed as to what tests have been performed?

"2. If the *Frye* test is adopted, what persons are to be considered in determining whether a technique has general scientific acceptance, those 'who would be expected to be familiar with its use' as held in *Commonwealth v. Lykus*, 367 Mass. 191, 203, 327 N.E.2d 671, 677 (1975), or some broader based group;
"3. If the answer to (1) above is 'yes,' is whether or not a given technique meets the *Frye* test a question of fact;
"4. If the answer to (3) above is 'yes,' by whom is the determination to be made;
"5. If the answer to (4) above is the 'trial judge,' then what is the basis for review of his decision, the clearly erroneous standard, abuse of discretion, or some other test;
"6. If the answer to (1) above is 'no,' then what standard should be used, that set forth in *McCormick's Handbook of the Law of Evidence*, § 203 at 491 (2d ed. 1972) ('Any relevant conclusions which are supported by a qualified expert witness should be received

What practical basis is a trial judge to use in determining whether a technique has general scientific acceptance? Will we now upon the basis of the language in the majority opinion be considering the view in a case such as this of one who has never done any experiments or testing in the field (such as Dr. Baker who did not even know that an examiner listened to each exemplar), and then adding up those opinions to determine that there is general scientific acceptance or a lack of general scientific acceptance?

We regularly permit eyewitness identification in court. Certainly voice is no more unreliable than eyewitness identification. See the documented instances of erroneous identification set forth by B. Wentworth et al., *Personal Identification* 26–27 (2d ed. 1932). For example, in one instance a man mistakenly thought a person he saw on a train was his good friend who had been the best man at his wedding. In another instance a person mistook a man he saw on a train for his college roommate.[28]

Upon close analysis it seems apparent that the majority can come up with only two "compelling reasons" for adopting the *Frye* test for this type of evidence. One is the jury's incompetence to evaluate expert testimony. The second "compelling" justification is to insure a minimal reserve of experts. The majority opinion states:

unless there are other reasons for exclusion.'), that stated by Thayer, *Evidence* 525 (1898) (whether in the judgment of the court, it will be helpful to the jury), or some other test?"

28. Critics who fear that scientific evidence has too great an impact on a jury to be admissible unless very highly reliable should recall that eyewitness identifications are certainly very impressive to a jury, also. It has been said, "The unreliability of eyewitness identification evidence poses one of the most serious problems in the administration of criminal justice." Note, *Did Your Eyes Deceive You? Expert Psychological Testimony on the Unreliability of Eyewitness Identification*, 29 Stan.L.Rev. 969 (1977). The remedy proposed by the aforementioned note was not exclusion of such testimony, but rather permitting opposing testimony by psychologists as to the unreliability of eyewitness reports.

"In addition to the advantage of substituting scientific for lay judgment as to scientific reliability, the court in *United States v. Addison, supra,* 162 U.S.App. D.C. 199, 498 F.2d at 744, pointed out that the *Frye* test '. . . protects prosecution and defense alike by assuring that a minimal reserve of experts exists who can critically examine the validity of a scientific determination in a particular case. . . . [T]he ability to produce rebuttal experts, equally conversant with the mechanics and methods of a particular technique, may prove to be essential.' "

I assume that they mean there should be qualified persons who can take issue with an expert's conclusion that a given exemplar is or is not the voice of the accused. (It must be remembered that this technique works both ways. It may clear an individual as well as convict him.) Such a minimal reserve obviously is available, as witness the list in the " 'Voiceprint' Defense Package" of the Practising Law Institute for its Spring-1974 workshop on advanced criminal defense techniques. They surely cannot mean a "minimal reserve of experts" prepared to joust on the issue of the validity of the technique itself. They have demonstrated that there are opponents to its validity, but carrying forward that philosophy would impede the introduction today of fingerprint or ballistics evidence because it is probable that a "minimal reserve of experts" is not available to testify in opposition to the use of such evidence as differentiated from testimony on the issue of whether the expert has drawn a correct conclusion from that which he has observed.

6. The appropriate standard

In the wake of the New Mexico Supreme Court's approval of the admission of polygraph evidence in *State v. Dorsey,* 88 N.M. 184, 539 P.2d 204 (1975), Professor Romero reviewed the standards for admitting scientific evidence under that state's new rules, noting, "The New Mexico and the Federal Rules of Evidence are essentially identical as they relate to scientific evidence." Romero, *The Admissibility of Scientific Evidence Under the New Mexico and Federal Rules of Evidence,* 6 N.M.L.Rev. 187, 188 n. 5 (1976). He began by examining Rules 702 and 703, pertaining to expert testimony. Federal Rule 702 provides:

"Testimony by Experts

"If scientific, technical, or other specialized knowledge will assist the trier of fact to understand the evidence or to determine a fact in issue, a witness qualified as an expert by knowledge, skill, experience, training, or education, may testify thereto in the form of an opinion or otherwise."

The Advisory Committee's Note includes this comment:

"Whether the situation is a proper one for the use of expert testimony is to be determined on the basis of assisting the trier. . . . When opinions are excluded, it is because they are unhelpful and therefore superfluous and a waste of time. 7 Wigmore § 1918."

Regarding this rule, it is said in 11 *Moore's Federal Practice* § 702.02 (2d ed. 1976):

"Since the finder of fact may give undue weight to expert testimony, 'because of its aura of special reliability and trustworthiness,' the rule continues the existing federal practice of limiting expert testimony by two standards.

* * * * * *

"Under this test the testimony of expert witnesses is acceptable where [1] the witness is properly qualified by his knowledge and where [2] his testimony will 'assist the trier of fact to understand the evidence or to determine a fact in issue.' " (Footnotes omitted.)

Referring to "the possibility that triers of fact may attach special significance to the testimony of an expert," it is said, "this seems unlikely where there are opposing experts." *Id.* at § 702.10 n. 4.

It will be noted that there is nothing in the rule which requires if the expert testimony is of a scientific character, that its underlying theories must be generally accepted by the scientific community. But

Romero points out, "By requiring that scientific evidence 'assist the trier of fact,' Rule 702 implicitly requires that the scientific or specialized knowledge that is the subject of expert opinion be *reliable.*" Romero, *supra*, 6 N.M.L.Rev. at 197 (emphasis added). This, he says, "is a question of relevancy to which Rule 401 is addressed." *Id.* at 198.

Federal Rule 401 provides:

"Definition of 'Relevant Evidence'

"'Relevant evidence' means evidence having any tendency to make the existence of any fact that is of consequence to the determination of the action more probable or less probable than it would be without the evidence."

Romero says, "Whether scientific evidence has any probative value, or, in the terms of Rule 401, any tendency to prove credibility [in the case of polygraph evidence], is the critical question." 6 N.M.L.Rev. at 201. Pointing out that this determination will turn on the reliability of the evidence, Romero continues:

"Reliability, however, is not a constant. It varies in degree ranging from minimal reliability to perfect reliability. . . . It is important, therefore, to determine to what degree the reliability of scientific evidence, in the sense that the underlying principles are valid, must be established before it is relevant and admissible." *Id.* at 203 (footnote omitted).

He concludes that the appropriate standard would be to require "foundation evidence tending to show that the scientific evidence is in *some* degree reliable." *Id.* at 204 (emphasis added) (footnote omitted). "Beyond this threshold, showing the degree of reliability would, of course, be a matter of weight for the jury." *Id.* at 204 (footnote omitted).

Romero concludes:

"In summary, the theory of admissibility for scientific evidence under the New Mexico and Federal Rules of Evidence is one of relevancy. First, scientific evidence must be relevant in order to be admissible under Rule 402. Second, there must be evidence tending to show that the scientific evidence is reliable in order to be relevant under Rule 401.

"It is submitted that the theory of admissibility embodied in the New Mexico and Federal Rules of Evidence is correct in its treatment of scientific evidence. Scientific evidence ought to be held to the same standard of relevancy as is non-scientific evidence. Although considerations of undue prejudice, confusion of the issues, or jury competence to deal with scientific issues may affect the decision to admit scientific evidence, these considerations do not and should not affect the theory of admissibility—one of logical relevancy. These considerations may, however, operate under Rule 403 to exclude relevant evidence, scientific or otherwise, whose probative value is substantially outweighed by these considerations." *Id.* at 204–05 (footnotes omitted).

It is obvious that the Federal Rules make no "express reference to a standard of general scientific acceptance." *Id.* at 206. The Maine court in *State v. Williams, supra*, said that the Maine Rules of Evidence (modeled on the Federal Rules) "do not purport to establish a special standard to govern the admissibility of testimony involving newly ascertained, or applied, scientific principles." Referring to the Federal Rules, Professor Romero points out that "probative value, can be established without demonstrating general scientific acceptance." 6 N.M.L.Rev. at 206. "Thus, a requirement of general scientific acceptance would appear to impose a more stringent condition for establishing relevancy—a condition that is inconsistent with Rule 401. . . . [E]vidence contesting the reliability of the results would merely affect the weight to be given the evidence." *Id.* at 206–07 (footnotes omitted).

Although no reference was made to Professor Romero's view, support for it is found in *State v. Williams*, 388 A.2d 500, where the Supreme Judicial Court of Maine said that the defendant relied on the fact that the Rules of Evidence of that state "do not deal *specifically* with the admissibility problem as it may arise by virtue of newness in the development, or application, of scientific principles." (Emphasis in original.) It said that the court was asked: "to fill this gap by establishing an additional precondition of admissibility as applicable *specially* to the situation in which proffered expert testimony will rest on a new ascertainment, or new application, of scientific principles—this further condition to be that there must be 'general acceptance' of such newly discovered scientific principle, or new application of scientific principle, in the relevant scientific field." *Id.* at 503 (emphasis in original).

The Maine court "refuse[d] to take th[is] course," saying it "believe[d] [this] would be at odds with the fundamental philosophy of [the Maine] Rules of Evidence, as revealed more particularly in Rules 402 and 702, generally favoring the *admissibility* of expert testimony whenever it is relevant and can be of assistance to the trier of fact." (Emphasis in original.)

Applying Romero's analysis to spectrographic voice identification, it would appear that there are sufficient indications of reliability to say that opinions based on the process are relevant. Critics of the technique admit that the process is "in some degree reliable." (Romero's threshold for admissibility.) The Bolt group said: "Under certain laboratory conditions and for some selected sample of the population, the probability of making an error in identification can be stated. [That rate of error is relatively low.] But for the less-than-ideal conditions encountered in forensic situations, the indications are that the probability of error will increase substantially." Bolt, Cooper, David, Denes, Pickett & Stevens, *Letter to the editor—Speaker identification by speech spectrograms: some further observations,* 54 J. Acoustical Soc. of Am. 531, 533–34 (1973). In essence, the critics have said that the reliability of this identification process under ideal conditions has been demonstrated satisfactorily; whether the process would prove as reliable under adverse conditions was something not proven by the Tosi study. The Bolt group's criticism and concerns cannot be read as stating that the process is totally unreliable. The Maine court in *State v. Williams,* 388 A.2d at 504–05, said:

> "[N]one of the acoustical scientists who testified questioned as facts that recordings of different human voices vary more in time, frequency and intensity than recordings of the same voice and that the spectrograph can accurately plot these variables. The opposition experts focused only on the difficulties of comparison and the exercise of judgment and the failure of the spectrograph experiments to account for many real world variables."

Certainly the limitations on the process should be considered by the trier of fact in determining the proper weight to be given this sort of testimony, but the limitations do not indicate that the spectrograph process is so unreliable that an opinion based on that process is irrelevant.

Professor Romero's view of the standard for admissibility of scientific evidence under the Federal Rules of Evidence, and the standard outlined by the Maine court in *State v. Williams,* 388 A.2d 500, are in accord with the cases discussed under part 2 of this opinion regarding ballistics and other scientific analysis, our prior Maryland cases involving expert testimony, and the standard put forth by Dean McCormick that "[a]ny relevant conclusions which are supported by a qualified expert witness should be received . . . ."

7. Conclusion

I conclude that even under the *Frye* test the trial judge did not abuse his discretion in permitting the opinion testimony based upon spectrographic voice analysis. Given the instructions which he gave the jury, I see no possible basis for believing that jurors would by this testimony in some manner become biased against the accused. I think it obvious that a "minimal reserve of experts" is available. I do not believe that jurors in Montgomery County are any less intelligent or well informed than the juries before whom I have tried cases. I have come away from jury trials with confidence that juries as a whole arrive at substantial justice. I concur 100% in the statement of Chief Judge Marbury for the Court in *Shanks*, 185 Md. at 449, 45 A.2d at 90: "Judges and juries must be presumed to have average intelligence at least, and no assumption to the contrary can be made for the purpose of excluding otherwise admissible testimony."

As I indicated at the outset, the majority opinion rests upon a rule criticized by eminent scholars, a rule which has never been adopted in Maryland. It not only is out of step with our prior decisions, it fails to apply the standards which respected courts have applied in the matter of opinion evidence concerning fingerprints, ballistics, and X-rays. It is out of step with the majority of reported opinions in the particular field with which we are here concerned, the most recent of which (*State v. Williams*, 388 A.2d 500 (Me.1978)) was decided only about two months ago.

We would do well to keep before us the observation of Judge W. Mitchell Digges for the Court in *Produce Exchange v. Express Co.*, 147 Md. 424, 446, 128 A. 403 (1925):

> "This Court in many instances has commented upon the inherent weakness of expert testimony, because of the fact that at best it is only an expression of opinion by the witness, and is in a measure usurping the function of the jury; yet in proper cases, when a witness has qualified by demonstrating to the court his peculiar knowledge of the question to be decided by the jury, and of which the average man would not have knowledge, this class of testimony has uniformly been allowed. The jury understands that the expert's testimony is not as to a fact, but simply his opinion as to the probable result flowing from facts which the jury might determine have been proven in the case. The opinion of the expert witness has probative force by reason of his unusual and expert knowledge of the subject, gained from study, experience, and observation. The worth of such testimony is based upon the logical inference that, if the witness' experience and observation have demonstrated that certain circumstances under certain conditions did produce a certain result, like circumstances under like conditions in other cases would produce a similar result. Having decided that this witness properly qualified as an expert, and that the questions propounded to him were proper hypothetical questions, the weight to be given to his answers was a question for the jury, with which this Court has no concern." *Id.* at 446-47, 128 A. at 412.

We likewise would do well to keep before us the view expressed by one of the "greats" in the field of evidence prior to Wigmore and McCormick in J. Thayer, *Evidence* (1898):

> "[T]here is ground for saying that, in the main, any rule excluding opinion evidence is limited to cases where, in the judgment of the court, it will not be helpful to the jury. Whether accepted in terms or not, this view largely governs the administration of the rule. It is obvious that such a principle must allow a very great range of permissible difference in judgment; and that conclusions of that character ought not, usually, to be regarded as subject to review by higher courts. Unluckily the matter is often treated by the courts with much too heavy a hand; and the quantity of decisions on the subject is most unreasonably swollen." *Id.* at 525.

I realize that the majority has purported to leave the way open for admission of testimony such as this at some time in the future. As a practical matter, however, what trial judge in his right mind would be so bold at any time in the future as to permit the introduction of such testimony when the Court has today rejected the very thoughtful and thoroughgoing analysis by Judge McAuliffe in this case as well as the equally thoughtful and thorough analysis by Chief Judge Gilbert for the Court of Special Appeals?

I am authorized to say that MURPHY, C. J., and ORTH, J., concur in the views here expressed.

Appendix 2.2

**Key Reporter Systems for the Federal Cases
and Their Abbreviations**

United States Reports	U.S.
Supreme Court Reporter	S. Ct.
United States Law Week	U.S.L.W.
Federal Reporter	F., F.2d, F.3d
Federal Supplement	F.Supp.
Federal Rules Decisions	F.R.D.
Court of Claims Reports	Ct.Cl.
Bankruptcy Reporter	B.R.
Reports of the United States Tax Court	T.C.
Military Justice Reporter	M.J.

**Key Reporter Systems for the State Supreme[16] Court Cases
and Their Abbreviations**

Alabama
    Southern Reporter   So., So.2d
Alaska
    Pacific Reporter   P.2d
Arizona
    Arizona Reports   Ariz.
    Pacific Reporter   P., P.2d
Arkansas
    Arkansas Reports   Ark.
    South Western Reporter   S.W., S.W.2d
California
    California Reports   Cal., Cal. 2d, Cal. 3d
    Pacific Reporter   P., P.2d
    West's California Reporter   Cal.Rptr.
Colorado
    Pacific Reporter   P., P.2d

Connecticut
  Connecticut Reports   Conn.
  Atlantic Reporter   A., A.2d

Delaware
  Atlantic Reporter   A., A.2d

District of Columbia
  Atlantic Reporter   A.2d
  Federal Reporter   F., F.2d

Florida
  Southern Reporter   So., So.2d

Georgia
  Georgia Reports   Ga.
  South Eastern Reporter   S.E., S.E.2d

Hawaii
  Hawaii Reports   Haw.
  Pacific Reporter   P.2d

Idaho
  Idaho Reports   Idaho
  Pacific Reporter   P., P.2d

Illinois
  Illinois Reports   Ill., Ill.2d
  North Eastern Reporter   N.E., N.E.2d

Indiana
  North Eastern Reporter   N.E., N.E.2d

Iowa
  North Western Reporter   N.W., N.W.2d

Kansas
  Kansas Reports   Kan.
  Pacific Reporter   P., P.2d

Kentucky
  South Western Reporter   S.W., S.W.2d

Louisiana
  Southern Reporter   So., So.2d

Maine
  Atlantic Reporter   A., A.2d

Maryland
  Maryland Reports   Md.
  Atlantic Reporter   A., A.2d

Massachusetts
  Massachusetts Reports   Mass.
  North Eastern Reporter   N.E., N.E.2d

Michigan
    Michigan Reports   Mich.
    North Western Reporter   N.W., N.W.2d
Minnesota
    North Western Reporter   N.W., N.W.2d
Mississippi
    Southern Reporter   So., So.2d
Missouri
    South Western Reporter   S.W., S.W.2d
Montana
    Montana Reports   Mont.
    Pacific Reporter   P., P.2d
Nebraska
    Nebraska Reports   Neb.
    North Western Reporter   N.W., N.W.2d
Nevada
    Nevada Reports   Nev.
    Pacific Reporter   P., P.2d
New Hampshire
    New Hampshire Reports   N.H.
    Atlantic Reporter   A., A.2d
New Jersey
    New Jersey Reports   N.J.
    Atlantic Reporter   A., A.2d
New Mexico
    New Mexico Reports   N.M.
    Pacific Reporter   P., P.2d
New York
    New York Reports   N.Y., N.Y.2d
    North Eastern Reporter   N.E., N.E.2d
    West's New York Supplement   N.Y.S., N.Y.S.2d
North Carolina
    North Carolina Reports   N.C.
    South Eastern Reporter   S.E., S.E.2d
North Dakota
    North Western Reporter   N.W., N.W.2d
Ohio
    Ohio State Reports   Ohio St., Ohio St. 2d, Ohio St. 3d
    North Eastern Reporter   N.E., N.E.2d

Oklahoma
    Pacific Reporter   P., P.2d
Oregon
    Oregon Reports   Or.
    Pacific Reporter   P., P.2d
Pennsylvania
    Pennsylvania State Reports   Pa.
    Atlantic Reporter   A., A.2d
Rhode Island
    Atlantic Reporter   A., A.2d
South Carolina
    South Carolina Reports   S.C.
    South Eastern Reporter   S.E., S.E.2d
South Dakota
    North Western Reporter   N.W., N.W.2d
Tennessee
    South Western Reporter   S.W., S.W.2d
Texas
    South Western Reporter   S.W., S.W.2d
    Texas Supreme Court Journal   Tex. Sup. Ct. J.
Utah
    Pacific Reporter   P., P.2d
Vermont
    Vermont Reports   Vt.
    Atlantic Reporter   A., A.2d
Virginia
    Virginia Reports   Va.
    South Eastern Reporter   S.E., S.E.2d
Washington
    Washington Reports   Wash., Wash.2d
    Pacific Reporter   P., P.2d
West Virginia
    West Virginia Reports   W. Va.
    South Eastern Reporter   S.E., S.E.2d
Wisconsin
    Wisconsin Reports   Wis., Wis. 2d
    North Western Reporter   N.W., N.W.2d
Wyoming
    Pacific Reporter   P., P.2d

NOTES

1. For a complete listing, see *The Bluebook: A Uniform System of Citation* (16th ed.). (1996).

2. Connecticut, Delaware, Maine, Maryland, New Hampshire, New Jersey, Pennsylvania, Rhode Island, Vermont, Washington, D.C.

3. Illinois, Indiana, Massachusetts, New York, Ohio.

4. Georgia, North Carolina, South Carolina, Virginia, West Virginia.

5. Alabama, Florida, Louisiana, Mississippi.

6. Arizona, Kentucky, Missouri, Tennessee, Texas.

7. Iowa, Michigan, Minnesota, Nebraska, North Dakota, South Dakota, Wisconsin.

8. Alaska, Arkansas, California, Colorado, Hawaii, Idaho, Kansas, Montana, Nevada, New Mexico, Oklahoma, Oregon, Utah, Washington, Wyoming.

9. *U.S. Law Week* is composed of two volumes; one provides current information about the proceedings and decisions of the U.S. Supreme Court, and the other summarizes legal developments in the federal and state lower courts and administrative agencies.

10. In fact, the *Federal Supplement* only publishes about half of the opinions rendered by the Federal District Courts. There are, however, looseleaf services that report some decisions that are not reported by the *Federal Supplement*. Some examples are *Federal Banking Law Reporter, Product Liability Reporter, Federal Securities Law Reporter, Trade Cases,* and *Fair Employment Law Reporter.*

11. When an appellate court "vacates" the lower court's opinion, it acts to annul or rescind the opinion. When it "remands" the case, it is sending the case back to the lower court for further action.

12. A "consent decree" is a judgment of the court that is formed with the consent of the parties. It is an agreement or contract of the parties by which they agree to settle their dispute fairly. Consent decrees are not published.

13. This is probable, but not always true. There are other occasions where the state is a party; for instance, condemnation proceedings.

14. The word *brief* can be used in another, more formal sense as well. Briefs are also the written documents attorneys submit to the court prior to trial that contain the arguments to support their respective positions.

15. Generally, see the pamphlet, *How to Use Shepard's Citations,* available in most law libraries.

16. New York does not refer to their high appellate court as their Supreme Court. It is known as the Court of Appeals. The New York Supreme Court is the state's trial court.

3

Finding Statutes and Legislative History

This chapter begins in the same manner as the last one, with the assumption that the researcher or practitioner already has the citation to a statute and would like to find the text. The goals of this chapter are to (a) help you locate the text of a statute, (b) help you locate the cases that interpret the statute, (c) describe the process whereby you can find the intent of the legislature (legislative intent) or the legislative history for that statute, and (d) describe the steps in checking the current status of any proposed bill in Congress or a state legislature. The first three goals involve one process, because when a statute is found, it cannot be assumed that its meaning can be determined from common or lay interpretations of the language used. Interpreting case law or construing a statute is an obvious way to look for this meaning, but it may not be available—that is, a court may not have considered the statute in question. Thus, it is often necessary to research the statute's legislative history to determine the legislature's intent when it is being enacted.

FINDING STATUTES

There are several features that both the federal and the state statutory systems have in common. These will be mentioned first before addressing the dimensions along which they differ.

A *slip law* is the first published official text of a statute. Most states as well as the federal government publish their laws in slip form after they are passed. Session laws are the next official form in which a statute appears. These volumes comprise chronological compilations of all laws passed during each session of the legislature. Each state publishes volumes called *session laws, acts and resolves,* or *laws* that contain all laws passed during that session of the legislature. The official session laws for the U.S. Congress are called the *Statutes at Large.*

FINDING STATUTES AND LEGISLATIVE HISTORY

Because the laws are arranged chronologically in the volume(s) containing the session laws, it is necessary to have them renumbered and reorganized (codified or arranged) by title or subject with obsolete or revoked laws omitted.[1] The code provides you with the text of the original legislation as modified by any subsequent amendments. Therefore, regardless of whether or not the legislature considered the same problem several times and passed several different pieces of legislation, the current law can be found in one volume. The official compilation for the federal laws is called the *United States Code* (U.S.C.). The names vary in the different states with their subject compilation being called the *Revised Statutes, Revised Code, Compiled Law, Consolidated Law, General Statutes, Statutes,* or *Code.* As with case law, there are unofficial compilations of state and federal statutes, as well as official versions. The unofficial versions reprint the statutes and contain annotations to cases that relate to them, as well as other editorial material that makes them a very useful research tool. Codes must be republished every few years to accommodate all the new laws that the legislature enacts. Between republications, they are kept updated with pocket parts in the backs of the hardbound volumes and by supplementary pamphlets.

The research tool that connects these volumes to the chronological session laws consists of tables of parallel citations found in most all volumes of both sets of these materials. In addition, referring from the code to the session laws volume is simplified by the fact that the session laws citation(s) is listed at the end of the comparable provision in the code.

If you have the citation to a statute, you may refer directly to it. In the event that you do not have a citation, each code has a descriptive word index, typically contained in separate index volumes that are part of the code. For example, the Michigan Polygraph Licensure Act can be found by looking in the index volume of the code under "Polygraphs." Although the indexing systems vary from state to state and state systems differ from the federal system, it is possible to find almost any act with a little persistence and to find the text of a statute, by knowing what the act is commonly called. The *Shepard's* citator series mentioned in the last chapter has a set called *Shepard's Acts and Cases by Popular Names: Federal and State.* By referencing the popular name of the act, the citation is easily obtainable. For example, the legislation in Michigan that is popularly called the "Forensic Polygraph Examiners Act" can be located by referring to that heading in *Shepard's*. It will show that the text of the act appears at Mich. Comp. Laws 1979, 338.1701 et seq. If *Shepard's Acts and Cases by Popular Names: Federal and State* is not available, or if you do not find what you need, most codes also have a popular name table in addition to its descriptive word index.

State Law

Most of the information needed to locate a state statute has now been covered. Appendix 3.1 contains the listing of state legislative materials and their abbreviations. Let us illustrate by using the previous examples. When you have a citation to the statute, the task is easy. For example, to find Michigan's Public Act 295 from 1972 (appropriately cited as 1972 Mich. Pub. Acts 295), look for Act 295 in the 1972 volume of *Public and Local Acts of the Legislature of the State of Michigan.*[2] Then use the table of parallel citations in the code, Callaghan's *Michigan Statutes Annotated,* to get the code citation: Mich. Stat. Ann. section 18.186(1). Once you have this citation, look for the volume of Callaghan's *Michigan Statutes Annotated* that includes Title 18 and section 186(1). Once in the code, make sure to consult the notes that are provided under the statutory provision. As mentioned previously, these notes contain citations to the cases that interpret and construe the statute. In addition, look for any supplements to the code and check to see if this statute has been revised or repealed. Finally, it may be useful to consult the *Shepard's Citator* series in connection with finding the subsequent citation history for both the statute and the related cases.

Although this approach is relatively straightforward, there are a few additional points that you need to learn.

Uniform Laws. There has been and will continue to be pressure to create statutory uniformity across the states on various topics. The impetus for this movement stems from the increased mobility of people and businesses and the confusion and higher compliance costs that result from conflicting state provisions. One result was the creation of the National Conference of Commissioners on the Uniform State Laws, established in 1892.

The National Conference of Commissioners on the Uniform State Laws is a quasi-official body with representatives from every state, the District of Columbia, and Puerto Rico. As stated in the organization's Constitution and Bylaws, "the purpose of the National Conference is to promote uniformity in the law among the several states on subjects where uniformity is desirable and practicable." The National Conference meets annually to consider drafts of proposed legislation. The drafts, proceedings, and other information can be found in the annual *Handbook of the National Conference of Commissioners on Uniform State Laws and Proceedings.*

The most successful of these proposed acts, prepared in conjunction with the American Law Institute, is the Uniform Commercial Code that has been adopted by every state. West Publishing Company compiles all the uniform laws adopted by at least one state into an annotated set called *Uniform Laws Annotated* (U.L.A.). The annotations contain commissioners' opinions about and explanations of these laws, as well as court decisions pertaining to them. The annotations also include references to law review articles, the *American Digest System, Corpus Juris Secundum,* and Westlaw Electronic Research. The set also has a pamphlet, the *Directory of Uniform Acts and Codes Tables-Index,* that contains a directory of the uniform acts, a list of each jurisdiction and the acts adopted, a cross reference index to the acts, and a list of the commissioners. The series is updated annually with pocket parts. This series and the *Handbooks of the National Conference of Commissioners on the Uniform State Laws* are handy research tools, if the research question concerns the position each of the states has taken on a particular topic, and if there is the possibility that uniform legislation has been proposed and adopted by several of the states.

Interstate Statutory Compacts. Occasionally, it is not uniformity but rather cooperation among the states that is considered desirable. States enter into written interstate legislative compacts to ensure mutual continued cooperation. These compacts are similar to treaties in their form and effect. Interstate compacts are found in the session laws of each state and in the *U.S. Statutes at Large.* Many are also found in each state's code. The Council of State Governments publishes *Interstate Compacts and Agencies* that lists compacts by subject with the year and statutory citations. However, the last publication of this reference was 1983.

For example, if you are interested in interstate compacts relating to surveying and maintaining state boundaries or more specifically, whether Michigan, Wisconsin, and Minnesota have such an agreement, the indexes to the respective state statutory codes under "Interstate Compacts" would indicate that Michigan does have such an agreement with Minnesota and Wisconsin, called the "Interstate Compact on Michigan, Minnesota, and Wisconsin Boundaries." The text of this agreement could be located at Mich. Comp. Laws sections 2.201 to 2.208 (1970), Minn. Stat. sections 1.15 to 1.17 (1980), Wis. Stat. section 14.82 (1975), and Pub. L. No. 844, 62 Stat. 1152 (1948). The last citation, Pub. L. No. 844, 62 Stat. 1152 (1948), is a reference to the *Statutes at Large,* the federal equivalent of session laws. All interstate compacts are published in the *Statutes at Large,* because the states are required to obtain the consent of Congress before entering into them. They do not become part of the United Stated statutes, however, and are therefore not published in the Categorical Compilation of U.S. laws or the U.S.C.

State Constitutions. If the research question requires information about a particular state's constitution, the best source is the annotated code of that state. It provides the most current text of the constitution and the references to other relevant materials, including court decisions interpreting it.

If the research question requires a comparison among the various state constitutions, then the most useful references to this material are the *Constitutions of the U.S.: National and State, 2d ed.,* published for the Legislative Drafting Research Fund of Columbia University by Oceana Publications, Inc. The set has an index called "Laws, Legislatures, Legislative Procedure: A Fifty-State Index" and "Fundamental Liberties and Rights: A Fifty-State Index." These volumes provide subject access to all the constitutions. The best source of information about an individual state constitution, however, is contained in the annotated statutory code of that state, because it not only provides the most current text of the constitution but also cites to court decisions interpreting it.

Rules for the State Courts. The law distinguishes between substantive and procedural laws. Whereas the former establishes the rights and responsibilities of parties, the latter establishes the manner in which these substantive laws can be enforced through the courts. In some states, these procedural rules are created by statute (e.g., California), whereas in other states, they are nonstatutory rules promulgated by the judiciary (e.g., Ohio). To complicate matters even further, in still other states these procedural laws are a combination of statutes and rules. Although most legislative services, both official and unofficial, publish the court-established rules along with the statutes, it is important to recognize that the materials you need may be rules, not statutes, and should be cited differently. Usually, these materials will include a statement that suggests the preferred citation style.

Federal Law

The U.S. Government Printing Office issues slip laws of the official text of laws enacted by Congress. Slip laws are designated by a public law number. As an example, for P.L. 101-336, the 101 stands for the 101st session of Congress, while the number 336 designates that piece of legislation as the 336th enacted by Congress during that congressional session. Slip laws are found at all libraries that are depositories for U.S. Government publications.

In Federal law, the official session laws are known as the *Statutes at Large*. These contain all public and private laws[3] and concurrent resolutions enacted by Congress, as well as reorganization plans, proposed and ratified amendments to the Constitution, and proclamations by the President, arranged chronologically by approval date with a subject index for each session. Public laws enacted since 1941 are also found in the *U.S. Code Congressional and Administrative News* (U.S.C.C.A.N.). They are published monthly in paperback form during the congressional session and cumulated in bound volumes at the end of the session. Note that important legislative histories (e.g., House Reports and Senate Reports) are included. A similar set is *Advance Sheets, United States Code Service*, which is published by the Lawyers Co-operative Publishing Company.

As with state session laws, research would be difficult if we had to rely on the chronological publication of the law. To solve this problem, the session laws undergo a process called *codification* that brings together all the current laws by topic (i.e., subject). Federal laws are codified into the official *United States Code* that provides access to the laws currently in effect. The U.S.C. arranges the public laws (not the private ones) that are still in force by subject in 50 titles (similar to chapters in a book) with separate index volumes. As a practical matter, most legal researchers do not use the official U.S.C. Instead, they use one of the unofficial codes that have extensive annotations: the *United States Code Annotated* (U.S.C.A.) published by West Publishing Company and the *United States Code Service* (U.S.C.S) published by the Lawyers Co-operative Publishing Company. These unofficial codes have extensive annotations that refer to legislative history, related law review articles, cases construing the provisions, administrative rules, and regulations promulgated to effectuate the statute, and appropriate forms to use when certain documentation is required. As before, the unofficial codes are very useful research tools, whereas the official code is, as well, official. Appendix 3.2 contains the listing of federal legislative materials and their abbreviations.

To illustrate finding a federal statute, consider the "Toxic Substances Control Act" (T.A.C.A.). Referring to *Shepard's Acts and Cases by Popular Names: Federal and State,* the citation to this law in the official United States statutory code is 15 U.S.C. sections 2601 to 2629 (1982). This citation could also have been found by looking in the index to the U.S.C. under "Toxic Substances." *Shepard's* also lists the corresponding citation to the session laws of Congress, the *Statutes at Large*: Pub. L. No. 94-469, 90 Stat. 2003 (1976). This citation can also be found at the end of the act in U.S.C. To find the text of the act, we simply refer to the volume of the U.S.C. containing provisions 2601 to 2629 of Title 15 or to page 2003 of Volume 90 of the *Statutes at Large*.

In addition to the *Acts by Popular Names* volume for both state and federal materials, *Shepard's* publishes a separate series of volumes for tracing the subsequent history of federal legislation. This series is called *Shepard's U.S. Citations: Constitution, Code, Statutes, Treaties, Court Rules Analyzed*. It provides citations to cases that interpret and construe specific statutory provisions, as well as citations to statutory amendments.

Rules for the Federal Courts. The U.S. Supreme Court has the authority to make rules for the federal courts. Federal court rules are found in many sources, some of the most commonly used of which are listed here. The text of the Federal Rules of Criminal Procedure is found in the appendix to Title 18 of the *United States Code,* together with annotations in the *United States Code Annotated* in five books following Title 18, and in the *United States Code Service* in a set of unnumbered volumes near the end of the U.S.C.S. The Federal Rules of Civil Procedure, the Federal Rules of Appellate Procedure, and the Federal Rules of Evidence will be found in the appendix to Title 28 of the *United States Code,* as well as with annotations in volumes following Title 28 in the *United States Code Annotated* and in the *United States Code Service.* The *U.S. Supreme Court Digest, Lawyers' Edition* has most of the major rules together with annotations to U.S. Supreme Court decisions. In addition, *Moore's Federal Practice Rules Pamphlet,* published annually in three books, contains many of the federal rules together with comments. Two major treatises that discuss this technical area need to be mentioned when researching federal rules: Wright and Miller's *Federal Practice and Procedure* and *Moore's Federal Practice.*

In addition to rules formulated by the Supreme Court, the lower federal courts are allowed to establish rules of procedure for their own use that meet their special local needs. These rules can be located in the following materials: U.S.C., U.S.C.A., U.S.C.S., Lawyers Co-operative's

U.S. *Supreme Court Report Digest, Lawyer's Edition,* Lawyers Cooperative's *Federal Local Court Rules,* and Callaghan's *Federal Rules Digest.*

CITATION STYLE

When citing statutory material, the rule is to refer to the current code in preference to the session laws, although it is common to list them both. When citing to the code, the law is generally listed by its common (i.e., popular) name if it has one, the title number where the law appears in the code, the abbreviation for the code, the section number, and the year in parentheses at the end of the citation. In descending order of preference, the year listed should be that appearing on the book spine, the year on the title page, or the latest copyright year. If the volume is a replacement of an earlier edition, then the replacement year and not the original should be cited. If the date that appears spans more than one year, then all the years should be given (e.g., 1976-1980). Finally, if the statutory provisions are located in a main volume and in a supplement, then it is necessary to cite both years (e.g., 1976 & Supp. 1993). For example, if you are citing to the federal Toxic Substances Control Act, then the code citation should be Toxic Substances Control Act, 15 U.S.C. Sec. 2601 (1988). This citation tells you that the federal Toxic Substances Control Act can be found in Title 15 of the *United States Code* at section 2601. The year on the binding of that volume is 1988. The citation to the session laws should include the name of the statute, the number of the public law, the volume number in which the law appears, the abbreviation for the session laws, the page number on which the law begins, and the year that it was passed. The appropriate public law number usually appears at the end of provisions in the codes and in the *Shepard's Acts and Cases by Popular Names: Federal and State.* There are also cross-reference tables in the codes and the *Statutes at Large* to provide the corresponding cites in the event that one citation is known, whether a public law number, code number, or *Statutes at Large* citation, but not the others.[4] For example, if citing to the federal Toxic Substances Control Act, then the session laws citation should be Toxic Substances Control Act, Pub. L. No. 94-469, 90 Stat. 2003 (1976). This citation tells you that the federal Toxic Substances Control Act has the public law number 94-469 (as the 469th bill passed in the 94th Congress), appears in Volume 90 of the *United States Statutes* at page

2003, and was passed into law in 1976. For more details about the nuances of citing to statutory material, see *The Bluebook: A Uniform System of Citation* (1996) and Dworsky (1991).

There is a distinction between cases and statutes that has particular relevance for the manner in which statutes are cited. Case opinions and the citations to them are written as a unit, notwithstanding concurring and dissenting opinions, because only those of the majority are binding legal authority. Statutes, on the other hand, are written in discrete sections with distinct purposes, each section having a legal weight that is coextensive with every other part. This is generally done so that in the event that one provision is declared unconstitutional by a court, it can be severed from the other sections in the act that would then be allowed to remain in force. With this purpose in mind, each of these discrete sections is given a separate number and so can be cited separately. To illustrate, the entire Michigan "Forensic Polygraph Examiners Act" would be cited as Mich. Comp. Laws sections 338.1701 to 338.1729 (1970), whereas the specific provision that pertains to the renewal of licenses would be cited as Mich. Comp. Laws section 338.1716 (1970). (Note that the Michigan code replaces titles by a decimal system.)

Finally as mentioned earlier, there are sometimes unofficial codes as well as official compilations of statutes. As with cases, citation should be made to the official code. It is often helpful, although not necessary, to include the equivalent unofficial citation as well, because there are instances in which the numbering systems are different. To illustrate this, the Michigan "Forensic Polygraph Examiners Act" found above in the official Mich. Comp. Laws at sections 338.1701 to 338.1729 (1970) can also be located in the unofficial Callaghan code where it would be cited as Mich. Stat. Ann. sections 18.186(1) to 18.186(29) or in the unofficial West series where it would be cited as Mich. Comp. Laws Ann. sections 338.1701 to 338.1729.

LOCATING LEGISLATIVE HISTORY

Because legislation is frequently ambiguous and contains omissions, the aforementioned techniques for finding cases that interpret or construe statutory provisions and amendments to the initial act are important to keep in mind. In many instances, however, case law is not sufficient, and it is often necessary to ascertain the intent of the legislative body when it passed the legislation. This is referred to as *legislative history*.

Legislative history includes such things as Presidential (or gubernatorial) messages, legislative hearings, debates, and reports, and earlier drafts of the final bill. These materials provide the best evidence of the legislature's intent, the best discussion of the problem that the legislature sought to remedy by passage of the act, and most crucially, the behavioral and social assumptions guiding the legislature's choice of particular provisions (Sales, 1983; Sales & Hafemeister, 1985). If, for example, the research entails an assessment of the law's effectiveness as a behavioral change agent, then legislative history is an invaluable aid for choosing the appropriate operational measures. Unfortunately, the extent to which these research aids are available at the state and federal levels differs enormously.

State Materials

It is very easy to describe the types of legislative history available for state laws, because there are few that are widely available.[5] Therefore, researching state legislation is much more difficult than researching federal legislation. Most states have a legislative service that provides information about a bill's progress prior to enactment or rejection, but these services are rarely available after the current legislative session is over. See Appendix A in the *State Legislative Sourcebook* (Hellebust, 1995) for the telephone number to call in each state to learn of a bill's legislative status. Committee reports and hearings are often not published and rarely available. Because the available materials vary tremendously from state to state, the best recommendation is to consult the clerk of the state legislative House or Senate or both, the state law library, or a legislative reference library (a governmental library that is operated for the use of the legislators) for the available information in the specific state of interest. A useful source for finding the legislative and administrative materials available in each state is the *Guide to State Legislative Materials, Fourth Edition* (Fisher, 1988).

Although not as desirable as official records, newspaper accounts of hearings and debates are a resource that should not be overlooked. In addition, consider requesting materials from the legislators instrumental in the law's passage and interviewing them, if this is at all possible. Although these resources are useful and informative, it should be kept in mind that both newspaper accounts from that time period and legislators' post hoc perceptions and memories may not be accurate and are not competent evidence of legislative intent.

Federal Materials

In contrast to the paucity of state documentation, there is a plethora of legislative history materials at the federal level. The following discussion describes the types of documents that are relevant to legislative history, explains the techniques for locating them,[6] then describes methods for obtaining the most comprehensive history for a piece of legislation.

First, it may be helpful to consider briefly how a bill is passed in Congress. The bill is introduced in the U.S. House of Representatives or the U.S. Senate and assigned a number that will follow it until it is passed or until the end of that session of Congress.[7] Subsequently, it is assigned to the appropriate committee. The committee may hold hearings on the bill, and if it decides to recommend passage, it will report it out of committee with a written recommendation to the House or Senate. Debates on the floor of the House or Senate may be held, and if approved, the bill will be sent to the other legislative body (House or Senate) for consideration. The same procedure will follow in the other legislative body. If the bill passes in both the House and Senate, it then goes to the President for his signature.

The political process virtually guarantees that many changes will be made in the provisions of a bill during the time between its introduction and passage. An examination of these variations over time can be most fruitful when trying to ascertain the intent of the legislators in passing specific legislation or to identify the behavioral and social assumptions guiding their choices of provisions. Deletions, additions, and other changes made in the language of the proposed legislation as it progresses through the different stages of the legislative process provide invaluable clues to the deliberations made by Congress.

Although the same bill may be introduced in both the House and Senate, it is important to note that the bills are numbered in series in both Houses of Congress as they are introduced. This process results in different House and Senate numbers for the same bill in most instances. Furthermore, the bill retains these numbers through an entire two-year term of Congress. Copies of these bills in microfiche are distributed to the U.S. Government Depositories. Therefore, bills introduced in Congress should be available in your geographic area. In addition, Commerce Clearing House provides subscribers with bills through its *Congressional Legislative Reporting Service.* Individual copies can also be obtained on request from the clerk of the House or Senate, the appropriate congressional committee, or the bill's sponsors in the House and

FINDING STATUTES AND LEGISLATIVE HISTORY 79

Senate. Similarly, the local offices of congressional representatives are often a convenient source of bills, because they are usually willing to obtain and send copies of bills to their constituents upon request.

Transcripts of the hearings conducted by House or Senate committees on topics under legislative consideration are an even more direct source of information on congressional intents and purposes than the bills. These materials are of value to the legal researcher, because the specific purposes of the hearings are to help Congress determine the need for legislation and to guide its members in the preparation of an appropriate law. The published record of these hearings includes not only the transcript of the testimony but also exhibits and other materials introduced by interested groups. Unfortunately, hearings are not held for all legislation, nor are all hearings published. When they are published, they are issued in separate volumes and generally identified by the name of the sponsoring committee, the session and Congress during which they were held, the title appearing on the cover of the volume, the bill considered, and the inclusive dates of the testimony. Although the volume may have a number, there is no uniform system in the numbering of the various series of hearings held by the committees. Hearings are listed in three sources. The *Monthly Catalog of U.S. Government Publications,* the most complete listing of federal documents, lists those hearings that are published during the time period covered by specific issues of the *Catalog.* Hearings are also indexed in the *Congressional Information Service/Index.* Finally, the U.S. Senate Library publishes the *Cumulative Index of Congressional Committee Hearings,* a retrospective index to hearings of both Houses arranged by subject, bill number, and committee. Copies of hearings can usually be found at law libraries and are available from the sponsoring committee or its members and the Government Printing Office.

In addition to holding and transcribing hearings, a committee recommending a bill for passage to the House or Senate drafts a report explaining the purpose of the bill and the committee's recommendations. These reports are then distributed to the entire House or Senate when the bill is reported out of committee. These reports are considered by many to be the best evidence of legislative intent. The reports are published in a numbered series and can be located if the number, session, and Congress are known. They are listed in the *Monthly Catalog of U.S. Government Documents* and the *Congressional Information Service/Index* and can be found at most law libraries. If the library does not have the report as a separate volume, check in the *U.S. Code Congressional and Administrative News* that reprints selectively chosen reports on major pieces of legislation. Occasionally, reports are available from the committees issuing them or from the clerk of the appropriate house, and many can be purchased from the Government Printing Office.

In addition to the congressional reports, there is also a series of congressional documents that includes some committee reports not included in the report series, presidential messages, communications from executive agencies, and special studies prepared at the request of Congress. They are identified by house, session and Congress, and document number. Documents are listed in the *Monthly Catalog of U.S. Government Documents* and the *Congressional Information Service/ Index*. To obtain copies, the sources are the same as above: libraries, the committees or the Clerk of the House, or the Government Printing Office.

Legislative history may also be found in congressional debates. These are printed verbatim in the *Congressional Record,* published each day that one or both houses are in session. In addition to the debates, the *Congressional Record* also includes exhibits and other materials in an appendix. A daily digest or index is published in each issue, cumulated every two weeks into a biweekly index. A bound edition of the *Congressional Record* is published at the end of each session and includes a cumulative index, a cumulation of the daily digest, and a history of bills and resolutions for that session. The bound set no longer includes the appendixes that appeared in the daily issues, although its index still refers to it. However, the appendixes are still available on microfiche.

Finally, when the President signs or vetoes legislation passed by both the House and the Senate, he often includes a statement explaining the purpose of the bill.[8] This, of course, only provides indirect evidence about the intent of Congress; however, it is useful background information. These messages are printed in several places: The *Congressional Record,* the *Weekly Compilation of Presidential Documents,* the *House and Senate Journals,* the *House and Senate Documents,* and on a selective basis since 1986, the *U.S. Code Congressional and Administrative News.*

Obtaining a Legislative History. Before beginning an extensive search for the legislative history of a particular act, you should query the law librarian about whether a compiled legislative history already exists (see also Johnson, 1988). Occasionally, a government agency or a commercial publishing house will publish in book form the entire legislative history of an important law. Thus, for example, the National Labor Relations Board has published what is regarded as an excellent

FINDING STATUTES AND LEGISLATIVE HISTORY 81

two-volume set on the Wagner Act, the Taft-Hartley Act, and the Labor-Management Reporting and Disclosure Act of 1959. If such compilations are not available, there are several sources for finding comprehensive federal legislative materials.

Perhaps the quickest way to obtain a listing of documents for the legislative history is to consult the statutory codes (i.e., *United States Code, United States Code Annotated,* and *United States Code Service*). The U.S.C. and the U.S.C.S. do not list the various items of legislative history; instead, they refer to the *Statutes at Large* that compiles the legislative history at the end of the statutory provisions.

West's *U.S.C.A.* cites its companion publication, *U.S.C.C.A.N.,* for a legislative history of the more major pieces of legislation. It is published in biweekly advance sheet form, as well as in cumulative volumes. It is useful because it contains the text of selected congressional documents in their entirety. Other services provide more comprehensive information about legislative actions, however. An act's coverage in U.S.C.C.A.N. begins with its total citation history, followed by a small selection of the referenced documents in their entirety. In addition to referring to U.S.C.C.A.N., the U.S.C.A. also publishes citations to court decisions construing the provisions, regulations promulgated to implement the act, and other library materials for each section of the act.

U.S.C.S., published by Lawyers Co-op, does not have a companion publication for legislative history, so like U.S.C., it cites to the *Statutes at Large*. It is similar to U.S.C.A., however, in that it lists additional references, such as court decisions, administrative rules and regulations, and law review articles.

An alternative way to obtain the legislative history of a bill is to consult the various status tables. These are published in a variety of materials. One source, for example, is the *Congressional Record* that biweekly publishes a table, "History of Bills and Resolutions." Although the fortnightly listings are limited in usefulness, because they do not cumulate throughout the legislative session, they are cumulated for each session and published in the bound index volume. This cumulated history is very helpful, although it does not contain references to hearings. In addition, the *Congressional Record* publishes daily a subject index for the Daily Digest that serves as a status table for bills acted upon. These too are cumulated by session into a separate volume containing the "History of Bills Enacted into Public Law." Compensating for the weakness of the former listing, this reference cites all hearings. Unfortunately, however, it has a weakness of its own in that it does not contain debate references.

Another daily congressional service, the *Congressional Monitor,* provides comprehensive coverage of all active legislation by reporting the various actions taken on proposed legislation, summarizing the current day's scheduled activity, and providing schedules of expected future activity. In addition, it provides short excerpts from selected congressional documents, weekly status tables of active bills arranged by subject, and a weekly list of printed legislative documents. Although it includes references to committee reports and hearings, it does not cite to debates.

The legislative calendars for the houses of Congress and the various committees contain status tables referring to pending business. The House of Representatives' *Numerical Order of Bills and Resolutions Which Have Passed Either or Both House, and Bills Now Pending on the Calendar* is particularly useful, because it is published daily in cumulative form and includes information on bills of both the House and Senate. In addition, the final cumulative issue covering both sessions of a congress comes out before the bound volume of the *Congressional Record.* It is not comprehensive, however, in that it does not include all bills introduced but only those on which action was taken.

The Library of Congress publishes a *Digest of Public General Bills,* but it is often not as useful as other publications, because it is only published eight to ten times a year. It includes summaries of public bills and resolutions and status tables of those public bills on which action has been taken.

In addition to the government publications, there are several commercial services. Commerce Clearing House publishes a looseleaf *Congressional Index* that is supplemented weekly. Among other information, it includes indexes on general public bills and enactments, status tables of active bills, lists of companion bills, voting records, and a list of pending treaties.

Another commercial service, the *Congressional Information Service/ Index,* is a looseleaf service that indexes congressional hearings, reports, and documents and compiles status tables for active bills. It is supplemented monthly with quarterly and annual cumulations. The annual cumulations are an excellent research tool, because they reference all pertinent legislative history for enacted legislation. This service provides detailed indexes to congressional hearings, reports, and other documents, as well as status tables of active bills. In addition, the monthly and annual cumulations contain the best summaries of hearings available.

A final commercial publication, the *Congressional Quarterly Weekly Report,* contains bill status tables arranged by subject for both houses, a cumulative index, and brief summaries of legislation and legislative news. Every year, an "Almanac" is published that summarizes the activities of Congress for the preceding year.

CHECKING THE STATUS OF PROPOSED LEGISLATION

State Bills

The materials available for checking on the status on proposed state bills vary from state to state. You would be advised to call the clerk of the legislature for information about the existing services in specific states. During the legislative session in Nebraska, for example, a legislative update is published weekly in a pamphlet form that provides the status of current bills. In addition, Nebraska has a toll-free number for a "legislative hotline" that also provides current status information. Finally in any state, newspapers—particularly the official state newspaper—provide accounts of current legislative actions.

Federal Bills

Because all the federal status tables described above are published first as looseleaf services of periodic reports, they are used not only in their cumulated form for tracing past history but also as they are issued to follow the current path of proposed legislation. In addition to the aforementioned resources, for the most current information, call the local office of your congressional representative and request the current status of the legislation.

Exercises

STATE

1. Where can the act popularly known as the "Anti-Liars License Act" be found in Kentucky Revised Statutes? What do this act's provisions cover?
2. Where can the act popularly known as the "Antiloafing Act" be found in New Jersey Statutes Annotated? Is this act still in force?
3. What is the act appearing at Mo. Ann. Stat. section 389.990 (Vernon 1949) popularly called?
4. Where in Louisiana's session laws would you find the original provisions of the act commonly called the "Crop Pledge Act?"
5. What do Ariz. Rev. Stat. Ann. sections 5-101 to 5-115 (Supp. 1974-1983) cover?
6. Where in Mont. Code Ann. do you find provisions dealing with "taking fish or game for scientific purposes?"
7. Is the Illinois "Foundling Act," Ill. Ann. Stat. ch. 58, section 1 (Smith-Hurd Supp. 1983-1984), still good law?
8. Where are the provisions for the "Michigan Sand Dune Protection and Management Act" in the Michigan session laws? What are the citations for this act in both Mich. Comp. Laws Ann. and Mich. Stat. Ann.?
9. The provisions at Okla. Stat. tit. 17, sections 41-47 (1953), are popularly known as what?
10. Where in the Wash. Rev. Code Ann. do you find the "Washington Poison Prevention Act of 1974?"
11. Chapter 106 of the Or. Rev. Stat. covers what topic? Or. Rev. Stat. section 106.060 (1981) covers what topic?
12. Where do you find provisions dealing with "strip and open pit mining" in the Tenn. Code Ann.?
13. The provisions appearing from N.M. Stat. Ann. sections 19-13-1 to 19-13-28 collectively refer to the "Lease of Geothermal Resources on State Lands." What is the popular name for these provisions?
14. Where in the Alabama session laws do you find the act that was codified at Ala. Code section 13A-7-23.1 (1982)?

FINDING STATUTES AND LEGISLATIVE HISTORY 85

15. Where in the Hawaii Rev. Stat. do you find the act popularly referred to as the "Prostitution Act?"
16. Where in the S.D. Codified Laws Ann. do you find the provision relating to the "qualifications of jurors?"
17. Conn. Gen. Stat. Ann. section 26-17a (West 1975) covers what topic? What is the popular name for this act?
18. Where in the Wisconsin session laws do you find the provision that repealed the act popularly called the "Hot Pursuit Act?"
19. Where in the Colo. Rev. Stat. do you find the provisions for the act popularly known as the "Headless Ballot Act?"
20. What do the provisions from Iowa Code sections 232.1 to 232.153 (1983) cover?

FEDERAL

1. What is the popular name for Pub. L. No. 91-596? Where does it appear in the U.S.C.? In the Statutes at Large?
2. What is the public law number for the Moss-Hennings Act? What is this act more commonly called? Where does it appear in the U.S.C.? In the Statutes at Large?
3. What is the corresponding cite in Statutes at Large for 29 U.S.C. section 201 (1976)? What is the common name for this act?
4. What is the corresponding cite in the U.S.C. for 91 Stat. 1566 (1977)? What is the common name for this act?
5. Pub. L. No. 95-91 establishes which department of government? Where in the U.S.C.C.A.N. would you find the legislative history of this act?
6. Where in the U.S.C.C.A.N. do you find the legislative history for Pub. L. No. 89-280? Under which title of the U.S.C. would you find this law placed?
7. What is the subject matter of 39 U.S.C. section 3010 (1976)? In what year was this provision passed?
8. What is the act at 10 Stat. 277 (1851-55) popularly known as? On what date was this act passed?
9. Which federal file of civil procedure covers the physical and mental examinations of persons? What title of the U.S.C. contains the rules of civil procedure?
10. Title 17 of the U.S.C. contains provisions on what topic?
11. Which provision of the U.S.C. covers "theft by bank examiner?" What is the corresponding cite for Statutes at Large?

12. Where in the U.S.C.C.A.N. would you find the legislative history for Pub. L. No. 95-541? What is the common name for this act?
13. Where in the U.S.C.C.A.N. would you find the legislative history on the National Swine Flu Immunization Program of 1976? What is the public law number for this act?
14. The U.S.C. contains a chapter on "Flood Control" that includes a section titled, "Emergency fund for flood damages; amount; commitments to be fulfilled by local interests." What are the U.S.C. and Statutes at Large citations for this provision?
15. Where in the Statutes at Large is the Federal Pure Food and Drugs Act found?
16. Where in the U.S.C. is the National Labor Relations Act found?
17. What is the public law number for the Kansas-Nebraska Big Blue River Compact Act?
18. What is the popular name for the act that appears at 12 U.S.C. section 1751 (1982)?
19. What is the corresponding Statutes at Large cite for 7 U.S.C. section 1422 (1982)?
20. What is the subject matter of 15 U.S.C. section 79c (1982)? What year was this provision passed?

Answers to Exercises

STATE

1. It is found at Ky. Rev. Stat. section 329.010 (1971). This act provides for the licensure of polygraphers.
2. It is found at N.J. Stat. Ann. sections 34:14-1 to 34:14-11 (West 1965). No, it was repealed by 1980 N.J. Laws 90, section 17, eff. Jan. 12, 1982.
3. It is popularly known as the "Bell Ringing Act."
4. They are at 1874 La. Acts 66 and 1922 La. Acts 93.
5. These provisions cover dog racing.
6. These provisions are at Mont. Code Ann. Section 87-2-806 (1983).
7. No, it was repealed by 1977 Ill. Laws 80-661, eff. Oct. 1, 1977.
8. These provisions are at 1976 Mich. Pub. Acts 222. The citations for this act are Mich. Comp. Laws Ann. sections 281.651 to 281.664 (West 1979) and Mich. Stat. Ann. sections 18.595 (1) to 18.595 (14) (Callaghan 1980). This illustrates the situation where the coding and numbering of two systems is entirely different. In the West system, whose numbering is the same as the official code, these provisions are in the chapter on "Lakes and Rivers," whereas in Callaghan, they are in the chapter called "Protection of Property."
9. They are known as the "Cotton Gin Act."
10. This act is at Wash. Rev. Code Ann. sections 70.106.010 to 70.106.910 (1975).
11. Chapter 106 covers "marriage." Or. Rev. Stat. section 106.060 (1981) covers "consent of parent or guardian if party under 18."
12. These provisions are at Tenn. Code Ann. sections 59-8-101 to 59-8-339 (1980 & Supp. 1983).
13. These provisions are popularly known as the "Geothermal Resources Act."
14. It appears at 1980 Ala. Acts 80-706.
15. These provisions appear at Hawaii Rev. Stat. sections 712-1200 to 712-1205 (1976 & Supp. 1982).
16. It appears at S.D. Codified Laws Ann. section 16-13-10 (1979).
17. It covers the "acquisition and preservation of tidal wetlands." This act is popularly known as the "Tidal Wetlands Acquisition Act."

18. It appears at 1980 Wis. Laws 324, eff. May 7, 1982.
19. These provisions appear at Colo. Rev. Stat. section 1-4-209 (1973).
20. These provisions cover "juvenile law."

FEDERAL

1. Occupational Safety and Health Act of 1970. It appears at 29 U.S.C. section 651 (1976) and 84 Stat. 1590 (1970-71).
2. Pub. L. No. 89-554. It is more commonly called the Freedom of Information Act. It appears at 5 U.S.C. section 552 (1982) and 80 Stat. 378 (1966).
3. 52 Stat. 1060 (1938). It is commonly known as the Fair Labor Standards Act of 1938.
4. 33 U.S.C. section 1251 (1976 & Supp. IV 1980). This act is popularly known as the Clean Water Act of 1977.
5. It established the Department of Energy. The legislative history appears at 1977 U.S.C.C.A.N. 854.
6. 1965 U.S.C.C.A.N. 3665. It can be found in Title 20, Education.
7. This provision covers the "mailing of sexually oriented advertisements." It was passed in 1970.
8. This act is popularly known as the "Kansas-Nebraska Act. It was passed on May 30, 1854.
9. Fed. Rules Civ. Proc. rule 35, 28 U.S.C. (1968). It is in Title 28, Federal Rules of Civil Procedure.
10. Title 17 contains provisions on copyrights.
11. It appears at 18 U.S.C. section 655 (1982) and 62 Stat. 728 (1948).
12. The legislative history appears at 1978 U.S.C.C.A.N. 4666. The common name for the act is the "Antarctic Conservation Act of 1978."
13. 1976 U.S.C.C.A.N. 1987. The public law number for this act is 94-380.
14. The cites are 33 U.S.C. section 701t (1976) and 62 Stat. 1182 (1948).
15. It is found at 32 Stat. 632 (1901-03), 34 Stat. 768 (1905-07), and 52 Stat. 1040 (1938).
16. It is found at 29 U.S.C. section 151 (1976).
17. Pub. L. No. 92-308.
18. It is commonly known as the Federal Credit Union Act.
19. 63 Stat. 1054 (1949).
20. It covers "exemptions regarding holding companies." The provision was passed in 1935.

Appendix 3.1

State Legislative Materials and Their Abbreviations

STATUTES

Alabama
    Code of Alabama   Ala. Code

Alaska
    Alaska Statutes   Alaska Stat.

Arizona
    Arizona Revised Statutes Annotated   Ariz. Rev. Stat. Ann.

Arkansas
    Arkansas Statutes Annotated   Ark. Code Ann. (Michie)

California
    *West's Annotated California Code   Cal. (subject) Code (West)
    *Deering's Annotated California Code   Cal. (subject) Code (West)

Colorado
    Colorado Revised Statutes   Colo. Rev. Stat.
    Colorado Legislative Service   Colo. Legis. Serv. (West)

Connecticut
    *General Statutes of Connecticut   Conn. Gen. Stat.
    Connecticut General Statutes Annotated   Conn. Gen. Stat. Ann.

Delaware
    Delaware Code Annotated   Del. Code Ann.

District of Columbia
    *District of Columbia Code Annotated   D.C. Code Ann.

Florida
    *Laws of Florida   Fla. Stat.
    Florida Statutes Annotated   Fla. Stat. Ann. (West)

[AUTHOR'S NOTE: An asterisk (*) appears beside the official code if one has been selected for those states with more than one service.]

Florida Statutes Annotated   Fla. Stat. Ann. (Harrison)
Georgia
   *Official Code of Georgia   Ga. Code Ann. (Michie)
     Annotated
   Code of Georgia Annotated   Ga. Code Ann. (Harrison)
Hawaii
   Hawaii Revised Statutes   Hawaii Rev. Stat.
Idaho
   Idaho Code   Idaho Code
Illinois
   *Illinois Revised Statutes   Ill. Rev. Stat.
   Smith-Hurd Illinois Annotated Statutes   Ill. Ann. Stat. (Smith-Hurd)
Indiana
   *Indiana Code   Ind. Code
   Burns Indiana Statutes Annotated   Ind. Code Ann. (Burns)
     Code Edition
   West's Annotated Indiana Code   Ind. Code Ann. (West)
Iowa
   *Code of Iowa   Iowa Code
   Iowa Code Annotated (West)   Iowa Code Ann.
Kansas
   Kansas Statutes Annotated   Kan. Stat. Ann.
   Vernon's Kansas Statutes Annotated
     Uniform Commercial Code   Kan. U.C.C. Ann. (Vernon)
     Code of Civil Procedure   Kan. Civ. Proc. Code (Vernon)
     Criminal Code   Kan. Crim. Code Ann. (Vernon)
     Code of Criminal Procedure   Kan. Crim. Proc. Code (Vernon)
     Corporation Code   Kan. Corp. Code Ann. (Vernon)
Kentucky
   *Kentucky Revised Statutes   Ky. Rev. Stat.
   Baldwin's Kentucky Revised   Ky. Rev. Stat.
     Statutes Annotated   Ann. (Baldwin)
   Kentucky Revised Statutes   Ky. Rev. Stat.
     Annotated   Ann. (Bobbs-Merrill)
Louisiana
   West's Louisiana Revised Statutes   La. Rev. Stat.
     Annotated   Ann. (West)
   West's Louisiana Civil Code   La. Civ. Code
     Annotated   Ann. (West)
   West's Louisiana Code of Civil   La. Code Civ.
     Procedure Annotated   Proc. (West)
   West's Louisiana Code of Criminal   La. Code Crim.
     Procedure   Proc. Ann. (West)

APPENDIX 3.1

Maine
   Maine Revised Statutes Annotated   Me. Rev. Stat. Ann. (West)
Maryland
   *Annotated Code of Maryland   Md. (subject) Code Ann.
Massachusetts
   General Laws of the Commonwealth
     of Massachusetts   Mass. Gen. L.
   Massachusetts General Laws   Mass. Gen. Laws
     Annotated   Ann. (West)
   Annotated Laws of Massachusetts   Mass. Ann. Laws
     (Michie/Law. Co-op)

Michigan
   *Michigan Compiled Laws   Mich. Comp. Laws
   Michigan Compiled Laws Annotated   Mich. Comp. Laws Ann. (West)
   Michigan Statutes Annotated   Mich. Stat. Ann. (Callaghan)
Minnesota
   *Minnesota Statutes   Minn. Stat.
   Minnesota Statutes Annotated   Minn. Stat. Ann.(West)
Mississippi
   Mississippi Code Annotated   Miss. Code Ann.
Missouri
   Missouri Revised Statutes   Mo. Rev. Stat.
   Vernon's Annotated Missouri Statutes   Mo. Ann. Stat. (Vernon)
Montana
   Montana Code Annotated   Mont. Code Ann.
Nebraska
   Revised Statutes of Nebraska   Neb. Rev. Stat.
Nevada
   Nevada Revised Statutes   Nev. Rev. Stat.
New Hampshire
   New Hampshire Revised Statutes   N.H. Rev. Stat.
     Annotated   Ann.
New Jersey
   *New Jersey Revised Statutes   N.J. Rev. Stat.
   New Jersey Statutes Annotated   N.J. Stat. Ann. (West)
New Mexico
   New Mexico Statutes Annotated   N.M. Stat. Ann.
New York
   *McKinney's Consolidated Laws of   N.Y. (subject)
   New York Annotated   Law (McKinney)
   Consolidated Laws Service   N.Y. (subject) Law (Consol.)

Colorado
    Session Laws of Colorado   Colo. Sess. Laws
    Colorado Legislative Service   Colo. Legis. Serv. (West)

Connecticut
    Connecticut Public & Special Acts   Conn. Acts (Reg. [Spec.] Sess.)
    *Connecticut Public Acts   Conn. Pub. Acts
    *Connecticut Special Acts   Conn. Spec. Acts
    Connecticut Legislative Service   Conn. Legis. Serv. (West)

Delaware
    Laws of Delaware   Del. Laws

District of Columbia
    *United States Statutes at Large   Stat.
    *District of Columbia Statutes at Large D.C. Stat.
    District of Columbia Register   D.C. Reg. (West)

Florida
    *Laws of Florida   Fla. Laws
    Florida Session Law Service   Fla. Sess. Law Serv. (West)

Georgia
    Georgia Laws   Ga. Laws

Hawaii
    Session Laws of Hawaii   Hawaii Sess. Laws

Idaho
    Session Laws, Idaho   Idaho Sess. Laws

Illinois
    *Laws of Illinois   Ill. Laws
    Illinois Legislative Service   Ill. Legis. Serv. (West)

Indiana
    Acts, Indiana   Ind. Acts
    Indiana Legislative Service   Ind. Legis. Serv. (West)

Iowa
    *Acts and Joint Resolution of   Iowa Acts
      the State of Iowa
    Iowa Legislative Service   Iowa Legis. Serv. (West)

Kansas
    Session Laws of Kansas   Kan. Sess. Laws

Kentucky
    *Kentucky Acts   Ky. Acts
    Kentucky Revised Statutes and   Ky. Rev. Stat.
      Rules Service   & R. Serv. (Baldwin)

APPENDIX 3.1

Louisiana
  *State of Louisiana: Acts of the Legislature   La. Acts
  Louisiana Session Law Service   La. Sess. Law Serv. (West)

Maine
  *Laws of the State of Maine   Me. Laws
  Acts, Resolves and Constitutional Resolutions of the State of Maine   Me. Acts
  Maine Legislative Service   Me. Legis. Serv.

Maryland
  Laws of Maryland   Md. Laws

Massachusetts
  Acts and Resolves of Massachusetts   Mass. Acts
  Massachusetts Advance Legislative Service   Mass. Adv. Legis. Serv. (Law. Co-op)

Michigan
  *Public and Local Acts of the Legislature of the State of Michigan   Mich. Pub. Acts
  Michigan Legislative Service   Mich. Legis. Serv. (West)

Minnesota
  *Laws of Minnesota   Minn. Laws
  Minnesota Session Law Service   Minn. Sess. Law Serv. (West)

Mississippi
  General Laws of Mississippi   Miss. Laws

Missouri
  *Laws of Missouri   Mo. Laws
  Missouri Legislative Service   Mo. Legis. Serv. (Vernon)

Montana
  Laws of Montana   Mont. Laws

Nebraska
  Laws of Nebraska   Neb. Laws

Nevada
  Statutes of Nevada   Nev. Stat.

New Hampshire
  Laws of the State of New Hampshire   N.H. Laws

New Jersey
  *Laws of New Jersey   N.J. Laws
  New Jersey Session Law Service   N.J. Sess. Law Serv. (West)

New Mexico
  Laws of New Mexico   N.M. Laws

New York
  Laws of New York   N.Y. Laws

North Carolina
   *Session Laws of North Carolina   N.C. Sess. Laws
   Advance Legislative Service to   N.C. Adv. Legis.
     the General Statutes of North Carolina   Serv.

North Dakota
   Laws of North Dakota   N.D. Laws

Ohio
   *State of Ohio: Legislative Acts Passed   Ohio Laws
     and Joint Resolutions Adopted
   Ohio Legislative Bulletin   Ohio Legis. Bull. (Anderson)
   Baldwin's Ohio Legislative   Ohio Legis.
     Service   Serv. (Baldwin)

Oklahoma
   *Oklahoma Session Laws   Okla. Sess. Laws
   Oklahoma Session Law Service   Okla. Sess. Law Serv. (West)

Oregon
   Oregon Laws and Resolutions   Or. Laws
       Or. Laws Spec.
       Sess., Or. Laws
       Adv. Sh. No.

Pennsylvania
   Laws of the General Assembly of   Pa. Laws
     the Commonwealth of Pennsylvania
   Pennsylvania Legislative Service   Pa. Legis. Serv. (Purdon)

Rhode Island
   Public Laws of Rhode Island   R.I. Pub. Laws
   Acts and Resolves of Rhode Island   R.I. Acts & Resolves

South Carolina
   Acts and Joint Resolutions,   S.C. Acts
     South Carolina

South Dakota
   Laws of South Dakota   S.D. Laws

Tennessee
   Public Acts of the State of Tennessee   Tenn. Pub. Acts
   Private Acts of the State of Tennessee   Tenn. Priv. Acts

Texas
   *General and Special Laws of the   Tex. Gen. Laws
     State of Texas
   Texas Session Law Service   Tex. Sess. Law Serv. (Vernon)

Utah
   Laws of Utah   Utah Laws

APPENDIX 3.1

Vermont
    Laws of Vermont   Vt. Acts

Virginia
    Acts of the General Assembly of   Va. Acts
        the Commonwealth of Virginia

Washington
    Laws of Washington   Wash. Laws
    Washington Legislative Service   Wash. Legis. Serv. (West)

West Virginia
    Acts of the Legislature of   W.Va. Acts
        West Virginia

Wisconsin
    *Laws of Wisconsin   Wis. Laws
    Wisconsin Legislative Service   Wis. Legis. Serv. (West)

Wyoming
    Session Laws of Wyoming   Wyo. Sess. Laws

Appendix 3.2

Federal Legislative Materials and Their Abbreviations

STATUTES

*U.S.C.	U.S.C.
[26 U.S.C. may be abbreviated as I.R.C.]	
U.S.C. Annotated	U.S.C.A. (West)
U.S.C. Service	U.S.C.S. (Law Co-op)

SESSION LAWS

United States Statutes at Large	Stat.

NOTES

1. Note that this system is different from that used for case law that exists in chronological form only. As noted in the previous chapter, the digests were devised as a means of providing topical access to cases.

2. Questions about proper citation style can be answered by referring to *The Bluebook: A Uniform System of Citation* (1996).

3. "A public law affects the nation as a whole, or deals with individuals as a class and relates to public matters. A private law benefits only a specific individual or individuals. Such laws deal primarily with matters relating to claims against the government or with matters of immigration and naturalization" (Jacobstein, Mersky, & Dunn, 1994, p. 152).

4. An ancillary rule for federal session law materials is that the citation to the *Statutes at Large* should be accompanied by the public law chapter number if the law was passed prior to 1957 and by the public law number itself if it was passed after that date.

5. In Nebraska, for example, the Clerk of the Legislature's Office has copies of legislative committee hearings and committee statements dating from 1937 and copies of

[AUTHOR'S NOTE: An asterisk (*) appears beside the official code.]

APPENDIX 3.2

legislative floor debates from 1961. In addition, there is a bill room that contains copies of all bills, both those introduced and those passed, dating from 1971 to the present. These are the only offices where these materials are available.

6. We will not describe the citation style for these materials, however, because the number and variety defy general rules that can be given succinct exposition in a book of this length. See *The Bluebook: A Uniform System of Citation* (1996) for the proper form for referring to these materials.

7. H.R. # = House Resolution #; H.J. Res. # = House Joint Resolution; S.B. # = Senate Bill #; S.J. Res. # = Senate Joint Resolution #.

8. These messages are also common when the President either signs or vetoes enactments.

4

Finding Administrative Rules, Regulations, Decisions, and Orders

This chapter introduces administrative law materials. It is an ambitious undertaking, because as explained in Chapter 2, administrative agencies have both quasi-legislative powers (i.e., rule-making authority) and quasi-judicial authority (i.e., the power to resolve disputes between parties by administrative decision of order). This dual authority results in two sets of materials that must be searched: administrative rules and regulations and administrative decisions and orders. We assume as before that the researcher or practitioner has the citation to an administrative rule or decision and would like to find the full text.

This chapter begins by describing the statutory provisions mandating public access to state and federal government information. Then a discussion follows of the research tools in administrative law with several examples used to demonstrate the steps necessary for answering administrative law research questions. We conclude with brief discussions of citation style and other sources for relevant information (e.g., presidential proclamations).

STATE-MANDATED PUBLIC ACCESS TO GOVERNMENT INFORMATION

Finding the names, addresses, and phone numbers of the heads of state agencies is easy. They are published in *The National Directory of State Agencies* (Wright, 1982). Finding state administrative law materials, however, is similar to finding state legislative history—it is not always easy nor are these materials always adequate. Because the states vary tremendously in their treatment of administrative matters, with some states providing better documentation than others, the best place for the beginning legal researcher to get an overview of administrative law in a particular state is to read the state's administrative procedures act (see Chapter 3 for details on how to find this statute). Although the specific provisions differ, most administrative procedures acts specify where proposed rules must be filed and published; what kind of public input (i.e., notice inspection and hearing) is required prior to the final adoption of a rule; what kind of procedures are necessary to revise or amend rules; what procedures are required to resolve disputes arising under administrative rules; what avenues of appeal from administrative decisions are available; and what kind of public access to these materials is available.

These acts are useful to the researcher or practitioner because of the information they provide about how to gain access to published rules and decisions. For example, Nebraska's act that appears in Neb. Rev. Stat. section 84-905 (1981) provides that "each agency shall make copies of the rules in force and effect for such agency available to all interested persons on request, at a price fixed to cover costs of publication and mailing; provided, any such agency may furnish the same without charge, in the discretion of the agency, if funds are available." It also provides that these rules are to be compiled, indexed, and published as the *Nebraska Administrative Code,* and that copies are to be distributed to the state library and to each county law library requesting a copy (Neb. Rev. Stat. section 84-906.03 [1981]). Finally, concerning the distribution of administrative decisions or orders, Neb. Rev. Stat. section 84-915 states that "a copy of the decision and order and accompanying findings and conclusions shall be delivered or mailed upon request to each party or his attorney of record." Thus, a copy of an agency's rules can be obtained from the agency, possibly at no cost, or examined at the state library or a county law library as part of a compilation of all agencies' rules.

As far as published administrative decisions are concerned, however, the statute is silent. It appears that there are no published or public sources of these documents. In addition, the statute does not mention an agency duty to provide members of the public with copies of decisions or the right to examine them. Even assuming that an agency would provide access to these documents upon request, research would be difficult, because there is no indexing system.

The Nebraska example is illustrative of the state provisions requiring government agencies to publish and otherwise provide public access to information, and most states have such policies in a broad capacity (Tseng & Pedersen, 1983). Although these policies are sometimes described in general terms in the Administrative Procedures Act, many states have separate statutory provisions that explicitly assure public access to government documents. These "freedom of information" acts are usually patterned on the federal Freedom of Information Act described below.[1] The variation among states makes it essential to consult the applicable statutory provisions within the state of interest. Appendix 4.1 provides a list of the available state administrative publications and their citation abbreviations.

FEDERALLY MANDATED PUBLIC ACCESS TO GOVERNMENT INFORMATION

As with the state materials, the best place for the beginning legal researcher to start exploring federal administrative law materials is the federal Administrative Procedure Act.[2] This law requires that proposed rules be published in the *Federal Register,* the official daily publication for administrative and executive documents, along with directions enabling interested members of the public to participate in the rule making "through submission of written data, views, or arguments with or without the opportunity for oral presentation."[3] To become a law, all final rules must also be published in the *Federal Register* at least 30 days before their effective date.[4]

In addition to the Administrative Procedure Act's publication requirements for rules, the federal Freedom of Information Act[5] requires that certain types of information be made available to the public. Agencies are required to publish in the *Federal Register* the following:

1. descriptions of its central and field organization and the established places at which, the employees (and in the case of a uniformed service, the members) from whom, and the methods whereby the public may obtain information, make submittals or requests, or obtain decisions;
2. statements of the general course and method by which its functions are channeled and determined, including the nature and requirements of all formal and informal procedures available;
3. rules of procedure, descriptions of forms available or the places at which forms may be obtained, and instructions as to the scope and contents of all papers, reports, or examinations;
4. substantive rules of general applicability adopted as authorized by law and statements of general policy or interpretations of general applicability formulated and adopted by the agency; and
5. each amendment, revision, or repeal of the foregoing.[6]

FINDING ADMINISTRATIVE RULES AND REGULATIONS 103

Each agency also has to make the following available for public inspection and copying:

1. final opinions, including concurring and dissenting opinions as well as orders, made in the adjudication of cases;
2. those statements of policy and interpretations that have been adopted by the agency and are not published in the Federal Register; and
3. administrative staff manuals and instructions to staff that affect a member of the public.[7]

Finally and perhaps most importantly, the act provides the following:

Each agency, upon any request for records which (A) reasonably describes such records and (B) is made in accordance with published rules stating the time, place, fees (if any), and procedures to be followed, shall make the records promptly available to any person.[8]

Thus, the act establishes a policy of broad public access to government information.[9] This policy is not without qualification, however; running counter to the mandate of disclosure is a band of narrow exceptions. Government agencies need not disclose information that is or are:

1. specifically authorized under criteria established by an Executive order to be kept secret in the interest of national defense or foreign policy and are in fact properly classified pursuant to such Executive order;
2. related solely to the internal personnel rules and practices of an agency;
3. specifically exempted from disclosure by statute;
4. trade secrets and commercial or financial information obtained from a person and privileged or confidential;
5. interagency or intra-agency memorandums or letters that would not be available by law to a party other than an agency in litigation with the agency;
6. personnel and medical files and similar files the disclosure of which would constitute a clearly unwarranted invasion of personal privacy;
7. investigatory records compiled for law enforcement purposes, but only to the extent that the production of such records would interfere with enforcement proceedings; deprive a person of a right to a fair trial or an impartial adjudication; constitute an unwarranted invasion of personal privacy; disclose the identity of a confidential source in the course of a criminal investigation or by an agency conducting a lawful national security intelligence investigation, confidential information furnished only by the confidential

source; disclose investigative techniques and procedures; or endanger the life or physical safety of law enforcement personnel;
8. contained in or related to examination, operating, or condition reports prepared by, on behalf of, or for the use of an agency responsible for the regulation or supervision of financial institutions; or
9. geological and geophysical information and data, including maps, concerning wells.[10]

Finally, 5 U.S.C. section 552a (1982), better known as the Privacy Act of 1974, protects individuals from unwarranted government disclosure of information that it may have about them.

Now that the requirements placed on federal agencies for disclosing information to the public have been described, we will turn to a description of the federal administrative law research tools.

FEDERAL ADMINISTRATIVE LAW RESEARCH TOOLS—RULES AND REGULATIONS

The major reference book for describing U.S. government agencies is the *Government Organization Manual* (1984). This federal publication is an annual directory that emphasizes information about the executive branch and the administrative agencies, although it does provide some information about the judiciary and Congress. It includes a listing or description of each agency, the statutes creating it as well as those statutes under its administration, its functions and authority, its predecessors, its current divisions and units, the names and functions of major officials, its organizational structure, and its major publications.

As mentioned earlier, the Administrative Procedure Act requires all agencies to publish their proposed and final rules and regulations in the *Federal Register.*[11] It provides a chronological text of these materials, each issue with its own subject index and two "Codification Guides." One Guide lists the regulations presented in that issue that represent revisions of past regulations, while the other lists the regulations that have been changed since the beginning of the month. In addition, an index is published at the end of each month. Finally, the Codification Guides are published in a separate volume at the end of the month, compiling the references to all changes in regulations since the beginning of that year. This last Codification Guide is usually shelved with the *Code of Federal Regulations,* described below, while the others are published as part the *Federal Register.*

The sheer amount of regulatory material and the frequency with which it needs revising make the *Federal Register* unwieldy to use as the main source of published rules and regulations. To alleviate the problem, Congress created the multivolume *Code of Federal Regulations* (C.F.R.)[12] The C.F.R. also contains all the current administrative rules and regulations but is organized by subject and divided into about 50 titles, some of which duplicate titles of the U.S. Code. For comparison purposes, the current C.F.R. and U.S.C. titles appear in Appendixes 4.2 and 4.3. The entire set of over 175 volumes with in excess of 105,000 pages is revised annually to include the text of new and amended rules and regulations as they exist on the first of each year.

The Codification Guides referred to above are based on the titles of C.F.R. and are the primary tools for locating changes in the current rules and regulations made during the year. C.F.R. also has an Index and Finding Aids volume that, in addition to a topical index, contains tables and cross references that allow one to change from one legal form to another. Thus, for instance, using the parallel references in the C.F.R. Index and Finding Aids volume, you can go from a statute to a related administrative rule by using the U.S.C. title and section to find related rules under C.F.R. Also, C.F.R. (see its Title 3) allows the use of the *Statutes at Large* citations to find related executive orders or proclamations and locate their full text in C.F.R. and the *Federal Register.* In addition, by examining a C.F.R. provision for an "Authority" note, you can find the statutory or presidential authority for the rule's promulgation. Finally, a "Source" note in a C.F.R. section refers to the *Federal Register* source for the regulation.

To find the most current version of a regulation, assuming that the citation is known, you would do the following: (a) check the Codification Guide List of Sections Affected (LSA) shelved with the C.F.R. that belongs to the most recent issue of the Code to see whether there have been any changes since the beginning of the year; then (b) use the *Federal Register* Codification Guides to see whether there have been any changes in the last month (i.e., since the last LSA was printed).

Imagine that you are interested in locating rules promulgated by the Department of Justice with respect to the confidentiality of subjects' responses for research conducted by the Department or on its behalf, but you do not know the citations. You first look in the Index and

Finding Aids volume of C.F.R. under "Research" and discover a citation to 28 C.F.R. section 22 under the subheading "Justice Department, confidentiality of identifiable research and statistical information." Picking up the volume containing Title 28, you find that section 22 is titled "Confidentiality of Identifiable Research and Statistical Information." The "Authority" note cites the Omnibus Crime Control and Safe Streets Act of 1968, 42 U.S.C. 3701 *et seq.*, as amended; the Juvenile Justice and Delinquency Prevention Act of 1974, 42 U.S.C. 5601 *et seq.*, as amended; and the Victims of Crime Act of 1984, 42 U.S.C. 10601 *et seq.* as authorizing the promulgation of these rules. The "Source" note refers to 41 Fed. Reg. 54,846 (1976). An inspection of the subsections reveals that several of them were amended by 43 Fed. Reg. 16,974 (1978), 45 Fed. Reg. 62,038 (1980), and 51 Fed. Reg. 6,401 (1986). A quick check in the LSA shelved with the C.F.R. and the Codification Guides of the *Federal Register* reveals that there have been no further changes since the beginning of the year.

A final step in conducting research on a particular rule or regulation is to check *Shepard's Code of Federal Regulations Citations.* This resource tells you whether it has been the subject of any judicial or agency interpretations. If you check the example, you will find that 28 C.F.R. section 22 (1983) has only been cited in one case, *In the Matter of Pittsburgh Action Against Rape,* 494 Pa. 15, at 24; 428 A.2d 126, at 130 (1981).

Now assume that you are interested in finding the regulations promulgated to implement a specific statute, such as the National Labor Relations Act, 29 U.S.C. sections 151 to 169 (1982). You should refer to the C.F.R. Index and Finding Aids volume and discover that these regulations appear at 29 C.F.R. sections 101 through 103 and 29 C.F.R. section 1420. Referring to 29 C.F.R. 101, you will find that 29 U.S.C. sections 151 to 169, together with the Administrative Procedure Act, are cited as authority for the regulations, and 52 Fed. Reg. 23,968 (1987) is cited as the source. You can select 29 C.F.R. section 101.2, "Initiation of unfair labor practices cases," to determine whether there have been any changes in it since the beginning of the year. By checking the LSA volumes shelved with the C.F.R. and the Codification Guides in the most recent issues of *Federal Register,* you will find that there have not been any changes. Finally, by checking *Shepard's C.F.R. Citations,* you will find that 29 C.F.R. section 101.2 has been cited in the following places:[13]

Section 101.2 et seq.
    356 F.2d 713 ^ 1966
Sections 101.2 to 101.16
    682 F.2d 772 * 1981
Sections 101.2 to 101.8
    620 F.2d 389 * 1979
Sections 101.2 to 101.7
    236 F.Supp. 29 ^ 1964
Section 101.2
    403 U.S. 303 ^ 1971
    421 U.S. 138 * 1974
    29 L.Ed.2d 492 ^ 1971
    44 L.Ed.2d 40 * 1974
    91 S.Ct. 1926 ^ 1971
    95 S.Ct. 1510 * 1974
    295 F.2d 329 ^ 1961
    297 F.2d 431 ^ 1961
    530 F.2d 615 ^ 1976
    86 Yale Law Journal 1381 * 1976
    96 Harvard Law Review 1976 * 1982
Section 101.2(b)
    691 F. Supp. 1295 ^ 1985
    284 F.2d 625 ^ 1961

FEDERAL ADMINISTRATIVE LAW RESEARCH TOOLS—DECISIONS AND ORDERS

Most federal agencies publish an official copy of their decisions and orders in a compilation similar to the official state reports of court decisions. These reports are published in chronological form with generally inadequate, noncumulating indexes and digests.

There is also an abundance of unofficial reporters in the administrative law area that specialize in particular topical areas (i.e., labor law and energy law). Most of these services quickly issue copies of agency adjudications in looseleaf form to their subscribers and, in addition, usually contain federal and state court opinions, new developments, and statutory and regulatory changes. Generally, their indexed tables of cases and cross references are superior to the official edition. These services provide the legal specialist, such as a labor or tax lawyer, with timely information about the most recent developments in his or her field from the entire spectrum of available sources. They are equally useful to researchers or practitioners interested in a specific substantive area of the law. A list of the official and unofficial reporters appears in Appendix 4.4, along with their citation abbreviations.

Shepard's has a number of special citator volumes for use in the administrative law area, such as *Shepard's Federal Occupational Safety and Health Citations, Shepard's Federal Labor Law Citations, Shepard's Immigration and Naturalization Citations, Shepard's Federal Energy Law Citations, Shepard's United States Administrative Citations,* and *Shepard's United States Patents and Trademarks Citations.* These volumes have extensive cross-reference tables that make obtaining both the official and unofficial citations to a particular decision quite simple.

Imagine that you want to find the text of a particular decision by the National Labor Relations Board, *Educational and Recreational Services, Inc.*, 253 N.L.R.G. 996 (1981). You should pick Volume 253 of the *Decisions and Orders of the National Labor Relations Board* and turn to page 996. If you know the N.L.R.B. citation but only have access to the unofficial services, you can go to the *Shepard's Labor Law Citations* and turn to the table of cross references going from official to unofficial reporters. There, you will discover that the opinion also appears at 106 L.R.R.M. 1058 (1981) and 1980-81 N.L.R.B. Dec. (C.C.H.) para. 17,767 (1981).

CITATION STYLE

In citing materials from the *Federal Register,* reference is made to volume, page, and year. Thus, 45 Fed. Reg. 62,038 (1978) refers to Volume 45, page 62,038 of the *Federal Register.* By contrast, C.F.R. is cited by title, section number, and year of volume; 28 C.F.R. section 22.1 (1983) refers to Title 28, section 22.1 of the 1983 issue of C.F.R. Finally, when citing to decisions and orders of agencies, list the name of the private party involved and the official reporter citation; that is, *Great Lakes Area Case,* 8 C.A.B. 360 (1947). Typically, these cases involve only one private party who is protesting an agency action; thus, listing the agency as the second party is unnecessary.

OTHER INFORMATION SOURCES

There are two other sources of information that we have not yet discussed—attorney general opinions and presidential documents. The U.S. Attorney General and the attorneys general of the various states issue formal and informal advisory opinions on various legal questions in response to questions from government officials. Although only advisory, they are given considerable weight by courts when interpreting statutes and regulations. These opinions are published in chronological volumes with indexes. Although most editions have indexes, they are variable in quality and are not cumulative across years. The *Opinions of the Attorney General of the United States* are listed in *Shepard's United States Administrative Citations*. The opinions of a number of the state attorneys general are listed in their respective state *Shepard's* citators, e.g., *Shepard's Wyoming Citations.*

Since 1965, presidential proclamations, executive orders, presidential messages, reorganization plans, treaties, and executive agreements have been officially published in the *Weekly Compilation of Presidential Documents*. In addition are the following:

1. Presidential proclamations are published in the *Federal Register, Code of Federal Regulations,* and *Statutes at Large*
2. Executive orders are found in the *Federal Register* and *Code of Federal Regulations*
3. Presidential messages appear in the *Congressional Record,* House and Senate Journals, House and Senate Documents and, on a selective basis, in the advance sheets of *United States Code Congressional and Administrative News* (U.S.C.C.A.N.)
4. Reorganization plans are published in the *Federal Register, Code of Federal Regulations, Statutes at Large,* and U.S.C.C.A.N.
5. Treaties and executive agreements have been issued in slip form and bound into the *U.S. Treaties and Other International Agreements* since 1950. Before that time, they appeared in the *Statutes at Large*

Exercises

1. What is the case name and reporter cite to the case appearing at 26 Fair Empl. Prac. Cas. (B.N.A.) 419 (1981)?
2. What is the case name and F.R.D. cite to the case appearing at 18 Fair Empl. Prac. Cas. (B.N.A.) 360 (1978)?
3. What is the case name and reporter cite to the case appearing at 10 Empl. Prac. Dec. (C.C.H.) par. 10,245 (1975)?
4. What is the case name and O.S.H. Dec. (C.C.H.) cite for the case appearing at 2 O.S.H. Cas. (B.N.A.) 3202 (1974)?
5. Find the F.2d, O.S.H. Cas. (B.N.A.), and O.S.H. Dec. (C.C.H.) citations for *American Petroleum Institute v. OSHA.*
6. What happened to *Certified Grocers of California, Ltd. and Eric C. Vaughan,* 227 N.L.R.B. 1211 (1977) on appeal?
7. What are the unofficial service citations for 587 F.2d 449 (9th Cir. 1978)?
8. Where in the Federal Register would you find 40 C.F.R. Sec. 707.60 et seq. (1983)? What is the effective date for this rule?
9. What information do you find at 45 Fed. Reg. 82,844 (1980)?
10. Using *Shepard's,* among other things, to assist you, what is the case name and reporter cite to the case in which 40 C.F.R. Sec. 434.20 was held valid?
11. Which edition C.F.R. does the case in question #10 refer to? How did you find this information?
12. Using *Shepard's,* among other things, to assist you, what is the case name and reporter cite to the case in which 20 C.F.R. Sec. 404.507 was held constitutional?
13. What is the cite to the lower court's opinion for *Nelson's Estate v. Commissioner,* 232 F.2d 720 (5th Cir. 1956)?
14. What is the name of the case appearing at 197 N.L.R.B. 363 (1972)? What are the corresponding unofficial service citations to this case?
15. 29 C.F.R. Sec. 1926.28(a) has been subjected to three constitutional challenges. What are the names, citations, and outcomes of these cases? Have there been any changes in the wording of the regulation since the Ninth Circuit held it void for vagueness in 1976?

FINDING ADMINISTRATIVE RULES AND REGULATIONS 111

16. What is the name and cite of the case that held 42 C.F.R. 435.723 (1978) unconstitutional? What is the Federal Register citation for this regulation? Has the regulation been altered since it was held unconstitutional?
17. What is the name of the case and the F.P.C. citation for Federal Power Commission Docket RP74-39-5?
18. What are the case name and the alternative citations to the case appearing at 5 Oil & Gas Rep. (MB) 808 (1956)? What are the citations to the lower court opinions for this case?
19. What are the name and the alternative unofficial service citations for the case appearing at 2 F.C.C. 2d 142 (1965)?
20. Before a new rule can be adopted, an advance notice must be published in the Federal Register stating the proposed changes and soliciting public comment. What is the Federal Register cite for the notice that preceded the adoption of 7 C.F.R. 102.27 (1984)?

Answers To Exercises

1. The case name is *Ali v. Southeast Neighborhood House* and it appears at 519 F.Supp. 489 (D.D.C. 1981).
2. The case name is *Rossini v. Ogilvy & Mather, Inc.* and it appears at 80 F.R.D. 131 (S.D.N.Y. 1978).
3. The case name is *Robinson v. City of Dallas* and it appears at 514 F.2d 1271 (5th Cir. 1975).
4. The case name is *Dennie's Contracting Co., Inc.* and it appears at O.S.H. Dec. (C.C.H.) par. 18,815 (1974).
5. The citations are 581 F.2d 493 (5th Cir. 1978), 6 O.S.H. Cas. (B.N.A.) 1959 (1978), and O.S.H. Dec. (C.C.H.) par. 23,054 (1978).
6. It was reversed sub nom. *NLRB v. Certified Grocers of California, Ltd.*, 587 F.2d 449 (9th Cir. 1978).
7. The unofficial service citations are 85 Lab. Cas. (C.C.H.) par. 11,001 (1978) and 100 L.R.R.M. (B.N.A.) 3029 (1978).
8. It appears at 45 Fed. Reg. 82,850 (1980). The effective date is Jan. 15, 1981.
9. The pages 45 Fed. Reg. 82,844-82,851 (1980) contain additional information about 40 C.F.R. 707.60 et seq., such as a summary, background information, a discussion of the underlying issues, and public comments. It also has a discussion about substantive versus procedural rule-making authority. The issue here was whether EPA has substantive rule-making authority under the Toxic Substances Control Act and if not, whether that would prohibit it from enacting the proposed rule. The issue was resolved by finding that the proposed rule was procedural rather than substantive and could be enacted pursuant to EPA's procedural rule-making authority.
10. 40 C.F.R. Sec. 434.20 was held valid in *Consolidation Coal Company v. Costle*, 604 F.2d 239 (4th Cir. 1979).
11. The case refers to the 1977 edition. The *Shepard's Code of Federal Regulations Citations* provides this information.
12. It was held constitutional in *Elliott v. Weinberger*, 564 F.2d 1219 (9th Cir. 1977).
13. The cite for the lower court's opinion is 24 T.C. 30 (1955).

14. The name of the case in *International Organization of Masters, Mates, and Pilots.* The unofficial service citations are 1972 NLRB Dec. (C.C.H.) par. 24,272 (1972) and 80 L.R.R.M. (B.N.A.) 1813 (1972).
15. The Ninth Circuit held it unconstitutional in *Hoffman Construction Company v. Occupational Safety and Health Review Commission,* 546 F.2d 281 (9th Cir. 1976), the 5th Circuit held it constitutional in *B & B Insulation, Inc. v. Occupational Safety and Health Review Commission,* 583 F.2d 1364 (5th Cir. 1978), and the Sixth Circuit held it constitutional in *Ray Evers Welding Co. v. Occupational Safety & Health Review Commission,* 625 F.2d 726 (6th Cir. 1980). No, there have not been any changes in wording.
16. It was held unconstitutional in *Herweg v. Rey,* 619 F.2d 1265 (8th Cir. 1980). The Federal Register citation is 43 Fed. Reg. 45,204 (1978). Yes, it was amended by 48 Fed. Reg. 39,629 (1983).
17. The name of the case is *Texas Eastern Transmission Corp.* and the citations are 51 F.P.C. 408 (1974), 52 F.P.C. 1851 (1974), and 53 F.P.C. 475 (1975).
18. The name of the case is *United Gas Pipe Line Co. v. Mobil Gas Service Corp.* and it can be found at 350 U.S. 332, 100 L.Ed. 373, 76 S.Ct. 373, and 12 Pub. Util. Rep. 3d (PUR) 112 (1956). The first opinion for this case appears at 12 F.P.C. 1422 (1953), and the appeal from that decision appears at both 215 F.2d 883 (3d Cir. 1954) and 6 Pub. Util. Rep.3d (PUR) 282 (1954).
19. The name is *American Telephone and Telegraph Co.* and it appears at 61 Pub. Util. Rep.3d (PUR) 562 (1965) and 6 Rad. Reg.2d (P & F) 535 (1965).
20. The notice appears at 40 Fed. Reg. 11,728 (1975).

Appendix 4.1

State Administrative Publications and Their Abbreviations

Alabama
   Alabama Administrative Code   Ala. Admin. Code

Alaska
   Alaska Administrative Code   Alaska Admin. Code

Arizona
   Official Compilation of   Ariz. Comp. Admin. R.
     Administrative Rules and Regulations
   Administrative Digest   Ariz. Admin. Dig.

Arkansas
   Arkansas Register   Ark. Reg.

California
   California Code of Regulations   Cal. Code Regs.
   California Regulatory Register   Cal. Reg. Notice Reg.

Colorado
   Code of Colorado Regulations   Colo. Code Regs.
   Colorado Register   Colo. Reg.

Connecticut
   Regulations of Connecticut State   Conn. Agencies Regs.
     Agencies

District of Columbia
   D.C. Municipal Regulations   D.C. Mun. Regs.
   D.C. Register   D.C. Reg.

Florida
   Florida Administrative Code Annotated   Fla. Admin. Code Ann.
   Florida Administrative Weekly   Fla. Admin. Weekly

[AUTHOR'S NOTE: Not every state has such a service.]

[AUTHOR'S NOTE: Because D.C. was granted limited home rule in 1975, cite to D.C. Mun. Regs. for acts of the new Council of the District of Columbia and to D.C.R. & Regs. for older acts.]

APPENDIX 4.1

Georgia
    Official Compilation Rules &   Ga. Comp. R. & Regs.
        Regulations of the State of Georgia
Illinois
    Illinois Register   Ill. Reg.
    Illinois Administrative Code   Ill. Admin. Code
Indiana
    Indiana Administrative Code   Ind. Admin. Code
    Indiana Register   Ind. Reg.
        Rules & Regulations
Iowa
    Iowa Administrative Code   Iowa Admin. Code
    Iowa Administrative Bulletin   Iowa Admin. Bull.
Kansas
    Kansas Administrative Regulations   Kan. Admin. Regs.
    Kansas Register   Kan. Reg.
Kentucky
    Kentucky Administrative   Ky. Admin. Regs.
        Regulations Service
    Administrative Register   Ky. Admin. Reg.
Louisiana
    Louisiana Administrative Code   La. Code
    Louisiana Register   La. Reg.
Maryland
    Code of Maryland Regulations   Md. Regs. Code
    Maryland Register   Md. Reg.
Massachusetts
    Code of Massachusetts Regulations   Mass. Regs. Code
    Massachusetts Register   Mass. Reg.
Michigan
    Michigan Administrative Code   Mich. Admin. Code R.
    Michigan Register   Mich. Reg.
Minnesota
    Minnesota Rules   Minn. R.
    Minnesota State Register   Minn. Reg.
Missouri
    Missouri Code of State   Mo. Code Regs.
        Regulations
    Missouri Register   Mo. Reg.
Montana
    Montana Administrative Register   Mont. Admin. Reg.
    Administrative Rules of Montana   Mont. Admin. R.

Nebraska
    Nebraska Administrative Rules   Neb. Admin. R. & Regs.
    and Regulations
Nevada
    Nevada Administrative Code   Nev. Admin. Code
New Hampshire
    New Hampshire Code of   N.H. Code Admin. R.
      Administrative Rules
    New Hampshire Rulemaking Register   N.H. Rulemaking Reg.
New Jersey
    New Jersey Administrative Code   N.J. Admin. Code
    New Jersey Register   N.J. Reg.
    New Jersey Administrative Reports   N.J. Admin.
New York
    Official Compilation of Codes,   N.Y. Comp. Codes R. & Regs.
      Rules & Regulations of the State
      of New York
    New York State Register   N.Y. St. Reg.
North Carolina
    North Carolina Administrative   N.C. Admin. Code
    North Carolina Register Code   N.C. Reg.
North Dakota
    North Dakota Administrative Code   N.D. Admin. Code
Ohio
    Ohio Administrative Code   Ohio Admin. Code
    Ohio Monthly Record   Ohio Monthly Rec.
                                                      (Banks-Baldwin)
    Ohio Government Reports   Ohio Gov't
    Ohio Department Reports (until 1964)   Ohio Dep't
Oklahoma
    Oklahoma Gazette   Okla. Gaz.
    Oklahoma Register   Okla. Reg.
Oregon
    Oregon Administrative Rules   Or. Admin. R.
    Administrative Rules Bulletin   Or. Admin. R. Bull.
Pennsylvania
    Pennsylvania Code   Pa. Code (Shepard's)
    Pennsylvania Bulletin   Pa. Bull.
South Carolina
    Code of Laws of South Carolina   S.C. Code Regs.
      1976 Annotated

South Dakota
  Administrative Rules of South Dakota   S.D. Admin. R.
  South Dakota Register   S.D. Reg.
Tennessee
  Official Compilation Rules &   Tenn. Comp. R. & Regs.
    Regulations of the State of Tennessee
  Tennessee Administrative Register   Tenn. Admin. Reg.
Texas
  Texas Administrative Code   Tex. Admin. Code
  Texas Register   Tex. Reg.
Utah
  Administrative Rules of the State of Utah   Utah Admin. R.
  Utah State Bulletin   Utah Bull.
Vermont
  Laws of Vermont   Vt. Laws
  Vermont Administrative Procedures   Vt. Admin. Proc. Bull.
    Bulletin
Washington
  Washington Administrative Code   Wash. Admin. Code R.
  Washington State Register   Wash. St. Reg.
Wisconsin
  Wisconsin Administrative Code   Wis. Admin. Code
  Wisconsin Administrative Register   Wis. Admin. Reg.

Appendix 4.3

United States Code (U.S.C.) Titles

1. General Provisions
2. The Congress
3. The President
4. Flag and Seal, Seat of Government, and the States
5. Government Organization and Employees; and Appendix
6. [Surety Bonds]
7. Agriculture
8. Aliens and Nationality
9. Arbitration
10. Armed Forces; and Appendix
11. Bankruptcy; and Appendix
12. Banks and Banking
13. Census
14. Coast Guard
15. Commerce and Trade
16. Conservation
17. Copyrights
18. Crimes and Criminal Procedure; and Appendix
19. Customs Duties
20. Education
21. Food and Drugs
22. Foreign Relations and Intercourse
23. Highways
24. Hospitals and Asylums
25. Indians
26. Internal Revenue Code
27. Intoxicating Liquors

28. Judiciary and Judicial Procedure; and Appendix
29. Labor
30. Mineral Lands and Mining
31. Money and Finance
32. National Guard
33. Navigation and Navigable Waters
34. [Navy]
35. Patents
36. Patriotic Societies and Observances
37. Pay and Allowances of the Uniformed Services
38. Veteran's Benefits
39. Postal Service
40. Public Buildings, Property, and Works
41. Public Contracts
42. The Public Health and Welfare
43. Public Lands
44. Public Printing and Documents
45. Railroads
46. Shipping
47. Telegraphs, Telephones, and Radiotelegraphs
48. Territories and Insular Possessions
49. Transportation; and Appendix
50. War and National Defense; and Appendix

Appendix 4.4

Official and Unofficial Service Reporters and Their Abbreviations

Abortion Law Reporter	Abortion L. Rep.
Accountancy Law Reporter	Accountancy L. Rep. (C.C.H.)
Administrative Decisions under the Immigration and Naturalization Laws	I. & N. Dec.
Administrative Law Reporter Second	Admin. L.2d (P & F)
Agricultural Decisions	Agric. Dec.
All States Sales Tax Reporter	Sales Tax Rep.(C.C.H.)
American Federal Tax Reports, Second Series	A.F.T.R. 2d
American Labor Arbitration Service	Am. Lab. Arb. Serv. (P-H)
American Labor Arbitration Awards	Am. Lab. Arb. Awards (P-H)
American Stock Exchange Guide	Am. Stock Ex. Guide (C.C.H.)
Antitrust & Trade Regulation Report	Antitrust & Trade Reg.Rep. (B.N.A.)
Atomic Energy Commission Reports	A.E.C.
Automobile Cases	Auto. Cas. (C.C.H.)
Automobile Insurance Reporter	Auto. Ins. Rep. (C.C.H.)
Aviation Law Reporter	Av. L. Rep. (C.C.H.)
Aviation Cases	Av. Cas. (C.C.H.)
Balance of Payments Report	Balance of Payments Report (C.C.H.)
Bankruptcy Court Decisions	Bankr. Ct. Dec. (CRR)
Bankruptcy Law Reporter	Bankr. L. Rep. (C.C.H.)

[AUTHOR'S NOTE: The following materials cover federal administrative agencies or a circumscribed legal area (e.g., labor and tax). Those covering a specific topic often include references to both state and federal materials.]

APPENDIX 4.4

Benefits Review Board Service	Ben. Rev. Bd. Serv. (MB)
Blue Sky Law Reports	Blue Sky L. Rep. (C.C.H.)
Board of Contract Appeals Decisions	B.C.A. (C.C.H.)
Civil Aeronautics Board Reports	C.A.B.
Code of Federal Regulations	C.F.R.
College Law Digest	College L. Dig. (Nat'l Ass'n College & Univ. Att'ys)
Collier Bankruptcy Cases, Second Series	Collier Bankr. Cas. 2d (MB)
Commodity Futures Law Reporter	Comm. Fut. L. Rep. (C.C.H.)
Common Market Reports	Common Mkt. Rep. (C.C.H.)
Computer Law Service Reports	Computer L. Serv. Rep. (Callaghan)
Congressional Index	Cong. Index (C.C.H.)
Consumer Credit Guide	Consumer Cred. Guide (C.C.H.)
Consumer Product Safety Guide	Consumer Prod. Safety Guide (C.C.H.)
Contract Appeals Decisions	Cont. App. Dec. (C.C.H.)
Contracts, Cases, Federal	Cont. Cas. Fed. (C.C.H.)
Control of Banking	Cont. of Banking (P-H)
Copyright Law Decisions	Copy. L. Dec. (C.C.H.)
Copyright Law Reporter	Copyright L. Rep. (C.C.H.)
Corporation Guide	Corp. Guide (P-H)
Corporation Law Guide	Corp. L. Guide (C.C.H.)
Cost Accounting Standards Guide	Cost Accounting Stand. Guide (C.C.H.)
Court of Customs Appeals Reports	Ct. Cust. App.
Criminal Law Reporter	Crim. L. Rep. (B.N.A.)
Customs Bulletin and Decisions	Cust. B. & Dec.
Decisions of the Comptroller General	Comp. Gen.
Decisions of the Employees' Compensation Appeals Board	Empl. Comp. App. Bd.
Decisions of the Federal Maritime Commission	F.M.C.
Department of the Interior, Decisions Relating to Public Lands	Dec. U.S. Mar. Comm'n
Economic Standards	Econ. Stand. (C.C.H.)
Education for the Handicapped Law Report	Educ. for the Handicapped L. Rep. (CRR)

EEOC Compliance Manual	EEOC Compl. Man. (B.N.A.)
Employment Practices Decisions	Empl. Prac. Dec. (C.C.H.)
Employment Practices Guide	Empl. Prac. Guide (C.C.H.)
Energy Controls	Energy Cont. (P-H)
Energy Law Service	Energy L. Serv. (Callaghan)
Energy Management	Energy Mgmt. (C.C.H.)
Energy Users Report	Energy Users Rep. (B.N.A.)
Environment Regulation Handbook	Env't Reg. Handbook (Env't Information Center)
Environment Reporter	Env't Rep. (B.N.A.)
Environment Reporter Cases	Env't Rep. Cas. (B.N.A.)
Environmental Law Reporter	Env. L. Rep. (Envtl. L. Inst.)
Equal Employment Opportunity Commission Compliance Manual	E.E.O.C. Compl. Man. (C.C.H.)
Equal Opportunity in Housing	Equal Opportunity in Hous. (P-H)
Exempt Organizations Reporter	Exempt Org. Rep. (C.C.H.)
Fair Employment Practices Cases	Fair Empl. Prac. Cas. (B.N.A.)
Family Law Reporter	Fam. L. Rep. (B.N.A.)
Federal Aid to Financing	Fed. Aid to Fin. (P-H)
Federal Banking Law Reports	Fed. Banking L. Rep. (C.C.H.)
Federal Carriers Cases	Fed. Carr. Cas. (C.C.H.)
Federal Carriers Reporter	Fed. Carr. Rep. (C.C.H.)
Federal Controls	Fed. Controls (B.N.A.)
Federal Election Campaign Financing	Fed. Election Camp Fin. Guide (C.C.H.)
Federal Estate and Gift Tax Reporter	Fed. Est. & Gift Tax Rep. (C.C.H.)
Federal Excise Tax Reporter	Fed. Ex. Tax Rep. (C.C.H.)
Federal Immigration Law Reporter	Fed. Immig. L. Rep.
Federal Labor Relations Reporter	Fed. Lab. Rel. Rep. (LR)
Federal Power Commission Reports	F.P.C.
Federal Power Service	Federal Power Serv. (MB)
Federal Register	Fed. Reg.
Federal Reserve Bulletin	Fed. Res. Bull.
Federal Rules of Evidence Service	Fed. R. Evid. Serv. (Callaghan)
Federal Rules Service, Second Series	Fed. R. Serv. 2d (Callaghan)
Federal Securities Law Reports	Fed. Sec. L. Rep. (C.C.H.)

APPENDIX 4.4

Federal Taxes	Fed. Taxes (P-H)
Federal Trade Commission Decisions	F.T.C.
Fire & Casualty Cases	Fire & Casualty Cas. (C.C.H.)
Food Drug Cosmetic Law Reporter	Food Drug Cosm. L. Rep. (C.C.H.)
Government Contracts Reporter	Gov't Cont. Rep. (C.C.H.)
Government Employee Relations Report	Gov't Empl. Rel. Rep. (B.N.A.)
Housing & Development Reporter	Hous. & Dev. Rep. (B.N.A.)
Income Taxes Worldwide	Income Taxes Worldwide (C.C.H.)
Indian Law Reporter	Indian L. Rep. (Am. Indian Law Training Program)
Industrial Relations Guide	Indus. Rel. Guide (P-H)
Inheritance, Estate & Gift Tax Reports	Inher. Est. & Gift Tax Rep. (C.C.H.)
Insurance Law Reporter	Ins. L. Rep. (C.C.H.)
Internal Revenue Code	I.R.C.
Interstate Commerce Commission Reports	I.C.C.R.
Interstate Commerce Commission, Valuation Reports	ICC Valuation Rep.
Labor Arbitration Awards	Lab. Arb. Rep. Awards (C.C.H.)
Labor Arbitration Reports	Lab. Arb. (B.N.A.)
Labor Cases	Lab. Cas. (C.C.H.)
Labor Law Reporter	Lab. L. Rep. (C.C.H.)
Labor Relations Reference Manual	L.R.R.M. (B.N.A.)
Labor Relations Reporter	Lab. Rel. Rep. (B.N.A.)
Life Cases 2d	Life Cas. 2d (C.C.H.)
Liquor Control Law Reports	Liquor Cont. L. Serv. (C.C.H.)
Media Law Reporter	Media L. Rep. (B.N.A.)
Medical Devices Reports	Med. Devices Rep. (C.C.H.)
Medicare and Medicaid Guide	Medicare & Medicaid Guide (C.C.H.)
Mental & Physical Disability Law Rep.	Ment. & Physical Disab. L. (ABA)
Military Law Reporter	Mil. L. Rep. (Pub. L. Educ. Inst.)
Motor Carrier Cases	M.C.C.
Mutual Funds Guide	Mut. Funds Guide (C.C.H.)
National Labor Relations Board Decisions	N.L.R.B. Dec. (C.C.H.)

National Public Employment Reporter	Nat'l Pub. Empl. Rep. (Lab. Rel. Press)
National Railroad Adjustment Board, 1st-4th Div.	(e.g.) N.R.A.B. (1st Div.)
National Transportation Safety Board Decisions	N.T.S.B.
Negligence Cases	Negl. Cas. (C.C.H.)
New York Stock Exchange Guide	N.Y.S.E. Guide (C.C.H.)
NLRB Decisions	NLRB Dec. (C.C.H.)
Noise Regulation Reporter	Noise Reg. Rep. (B.N.A.)
Nuclear Regulation Reporter	Nuclear Reg. Rep. (C.C.H.)
Nuclear Regulatory Commission	NRC
Occupational Safety & Health Cases	O.S.H. Cas. (B.N.A.)
Occupational Safety & Health Decisions	O.S.H. Dec. (C.C.H.)
Occupational Safety & Health Reporter	O.S.H. Rep. (B.N.A.)
Official Gazette of the United States Patent Office	Off. Gaz. Pat. Office
Official Opinions of the Solicitor for the Post Office Department	Op. Solic. P.O. Dep't
Oil & Gas Reporter	Oil & Gas Rep. (P-H)
Opinions of the Attorney General	Op. Att. Gen.
Opinions of the Office of Legal Counsel	Op. Off. Legal Counsel
Patents, Decisions of the Commissioner and of U.S. Courts	Dec. Comm'r Pat.
Patents, Trademark & Copyright Journal	Pat. Trademark & Copyright J. (B.N.A.)
Pension & Profit Sharing	Pens. & Profit Sharing (P-H)
Pension Plan Guide	Pens. Plan Guide (C.C.H.)
Pension Reporter	Pens. Rep. (B.N.A.)
Pollution Control Guide	Pollution Cont. Guide (C.C.H.)
Poverty Law Reporter	Pov. L. Rep. (C.C.H.)
Private Foundations Reporter	Priv. Found. Rep. (C.C.H.)
Product Safety & Liability Reporter	Prod. Safety & Liab. Rep. (B.N.A.)
Products Liability Reports	Prod. Liab. Rep. (C.C.H.)
Public Bargaining Cases	Pub. Bargaining Cas. (C.C.H.)
Public Employee Bargaining	Pub. Employee Bargaining (C.C.H.)

Public Utilities Reports	Pub. Util. Rep. (PUR)
Radio Regulation	Rad. Reg. (P & F)
School Law Reporter	School L. Rep. (Nat'l Org. on Legal Probs. in Educ.)
Search & Seizure Bulletin	Search & Seizure Bull. (Quinlan)
SEC Accounting Rules	SEC Accounting R. (C.C.H.)
Secured Transactions Guide	Secured Transactions Guide (C.C.H.)
Securities and Exchange Commission Decisions and Reports	S.E.C.
Securities & Federal Corporate Law Report	Sec. & Fed. Corp. L. Rep. (Clark Boardman)
Securities Regulation Guide	Sec. Reg. Guide (P-H)
Securities Regulation & Law Report	Sec. Reg. & L. Rep. (B.N.A.)
Selective Service Law Reporter Educ.	Sel. Serv. L. Rep. (Pub. L. Inst.)
Standard Excess Profits Tax Reporter	Stand. Ex. Prof. Tax Rep. (C.C.H.)
Standard Federal Tax Reporter	Stand. Ex. Tax Rep. (C.C.H.)
State and Local Tax Service	St. & Loc. Tax Serv. (P-H)
State and Local Taxes	St. & Loc. Taxes (B.N.A.)
State Motor Carrier Guide	St. Mot. Carr. Guide (C.C.H.)
State Tax Cases	St. Tax Cas. (C.C.H.)
State Tax Cases Reports	St. Tax Cas. Rep. (C.C.H.)
State Tax Reports	St. Tax Rep. (C.C.H.)
Tax Court Memorandum Decisions	Tax Ct. Mem. Dec.(C.C.H.) or (P-H)
Tax Court Reported Decisions	Tax Ct. Rep. Dec. (P-H)
Tax Court Reports	Tax Ct. Rep. (C.C.H.)
Tax Management	Tax Mgmt. (B.N.A.)
Tax Treaties	Tax Treaties (C.C.H.)
Trade Cases	Trade Cas. (C.C.H.)
Trade Regulation Reporter	Trade Reg. Rep. (C.C.H.)
Treasury Decisions Under Customs and Other Laws	Treas. Dec.
Treasury Decisions Under Internal Revenue Laws	Treas. Dec. Int. Rev.
Treasury Regulations	Treas. Reg.
Unemployment Insurance Reports	Unempl. Ins. Rep. (C.C.H.)

Uniform Commercial Code Reporting Service	U.C.C. Rep. Serv. (Callaghan)
United States Law Week	U.S.L.W. (B.N.A.—publisher need not be indicated)
United States Patents Quarterly	U.S.P.Q. (B.N.A.)
Urban Affairs Reporter	Urb. Aff. Rep. (C.C.H.)
U.S. Supreme Court Bulletin	S. Ct. Bull. (C.C.H.)
U.S. Tax Cases	U.S. Tax Cas. (C.C.H.)
Wage and Hour Cases	Wage & Hour Cas. (B.N.A.)
Washington Financial Reports	Wash. Fin. Rep. (B.N.A.)
Wills, Estates and Trust Service	Wills Est. & Tr. Serv. (P-H)
Workmen's Compensation Law Reports	Workmen's Comp. L. Rep. (C.C.H.)

NOTES

1. For information about the various state provisions in this area, see Thurman (1973).
2. 5 U.S.C. sections 551-559, 701-706 (1982).
3. 5 U.S.C. section 553(b)-553(c) (1982).
4. 5 U.S.C. section 553(d) (1982).
5. 5 U.S.C. section 552 (1982).
6. 5 U.S.C. section 552(a)(1) (1982).
7. 5 U.S.C. section 552(a)(2) (1982).
8. 5 U.S.C. section 552(a)(3) (1982).
9. The federal Freedom of Information Act has serious implications for federally funded researchers with respect to their property interests in their data and the degree of confidentiality that they can provide their subjects. FOIA requires grant proposals, contracts, raw data, preliminary analyses, and final reports to be disclosed if requested unless they fit under the categories of exempt information. This is not without potential benefits, however, in that unfunded researchers may obtain copies of funded proposals and use them to learn to write better proposals. For a full discussion of these issues, see Morris, Sales, and Berman (1981).
10. 5 U.S.C. section 552(b) (1982).
11. The *Federal Register* was established as a daily publication for administrative and executive documents by the Federal Register Act, ch. 417, 49 Stat. 500 (1935).
12. Ch. 369, 50 Stat. 304 (1937).
13. An * followed by a year refers to the C.F.R. edition cited. If an edition is not cited, a ^ followed by a year refers to the date of the citing reference.

Epilogue

By reaching this point, you have covered a tremendous amount of information. Indeed, it may have seemed overwhelming. Like any new skill, however, practice will make perfect. You may want to repeat going through the volume and redoing the exercises one or more times. Then branch out to other legal questions and issues. It is critical, however, that you use your new knowledge sufficiently and regularly so that it does not atrophy. Doing so will benefit you, the readers of your scholarly manuscripts, and your clients!

Finally, we encourage you to be playful in your legal research. Time spent looking at cases or treatises that are related to your topic or concern but are not on point may suggest new research issues, legal research techniques, or areas of practice. Be creative and have fun discovering a new universe of information.

References

American jurisprudence legal forms (2nd ed.). (1994). New York: Lawyers Co-operative.
American Psychological Association. (1995). *Publication manual of American Psychological Association* (4th ed.). Washington, DC: Author.
Black, H. C. (1990). *Black's law dictionary: Definitions of the terms and phrases of American and English jurisprudence, ancient and modern* (6th ed.). St. Paul, MN: West.
The bluebook: A uniform system of citation (16th ed.). (1996). Cambridge, MA: Harvard Law Review Association.
Cohen, M. L. (1992). *Legal research in a nutshell* (5th ed.). St. Paul, MN: West.
Cohen, M. L., Berring, R. C., & Olson, K. C. (1989). *How to find the law* (9th ed.). St. Paul, MN: West.
Columbia University. (1962). *Constitutions of the United States: National and State* (2nd ed.) Dobbs Ferry, NY: Oceana.
Dunn, P. (1977). Unreported decisions in the United States Courts of Appeals. *Cornell Law Review, 63,* 128-148.
Dworsky, (1991). *User's guide to the bluebook.* Littleton, CO: F. B. Rothman.
Fisher, M. L. (1988). *Guide to state legislative materials* (4th ed.). Littleton, CO: F. B. Rothman.
Gerstein, R. S. (1984). "Law by elimination": Depublication in the California Supreme Court. *Judicature, 67,* 292-298.
Government organization manual. (1984). Washington, DC: Government Printing Office.
Hellebust, L. (1995). *State legislative sourcebook 1992: A resource guide to legislative information in the fifty states.* Topeka, KS: Government Research Service.
Jacobstein, J. M., Mersky, R. M., & Dunn, D. J. (1994). *Fundamentals of legal research* (5th ed.). New York: Foundation Press.
Johnson, N. P. (1988). *Sources of compiled legislative histories: A bibliography of government documents, periodical articles, and books. 1st Congress—99th Congress.* Littleton, CO: F. B. Rothman.
Lieberson, A. D. (1990). *West's legal forms* (Rev. 2nd ed.). St. Paul, MN: West.
Morris, R. A., Sales, B. D., & Berman, J. J. (1981). Research and the Freedom of Information Act. *American Psychologist, 36,* 819-826.
Price, M. O., Bitner, H., & Bysiewicz, S. (1979). *Effective legal research* (4th ed.). Boston: Little, Brown.
Reynolds, W. L., & Richman, W. M. (1978). The non-precedential precedent—Limited publication and no-citation rules in the United States Courts of Appeals. *Columbia Law Review, 78,* 1167-1208.
Sales, B. D. (1983). The legal regulation of psychology: Professional and scientific interaction. In C. J. Scheirer & B. L. Hammonds (Eds.), *The master lecture series. Vol. 2: Psychology and the law* (pp. 5-36). Washington, DC: American Psychological Association.

REFERENCES

Sales, B. D., & Hafemeister, T. (1985). Law and psychology. In E. Altmaier & M. Meyer (Eds.), *Applied specialties in psychology* (pp. 331-373). New York: Random House.

Sand, L. B. (1984) *Model federal jury instructions: Criminal & civil.* New York: Mathew Bender.

Shuchman, P., & Gelfand, A. (1980). The use of Local Rule 21 in the Fifth Circuit: Can judges select cases of "no precedential value"? *Emory Law Journal, 29,* 195-230.

Thurman, S. D. (1973). *The right of access to information from the government.* New York: Oceana.

Tseng, H. P., & Pedersen, D. B. (1983). Acquisition of state administrative rules and regulations—Update 1983. *Administrative Law Review, 35,* 349-389.

Weihofen, H. (1980). *Legal writing style* (2nd ed.). St. Paul, MN: West.

Wright, N. D. (1982). *The National Directory of State Agencies.* Arlington, VA: Information Resources Press.

Supplementary Reading

Ballentine, J. A. (1969). *Ballentine's law dictionary, with pronunciations* (3rd ed.). New York: Lawyers Co-operative.

Biskind, E. L. (1971). *Legal writing simplified.* New York: Clark Boardman.

Brand, N., & White, J. O. (1994). *Legal writing: The strategy of persuasion* (3rd ed.). New York: St. Martin's.

Foster, L., & Boast, C. (1981). *Subject compilations of state laws: Research guide and annotated bibliography* (2nd ed.). Westport, CT: Greenwood.

Goehlert, R. U., & Martin, F. S. (1979). *Congress and law-making: Researching the legislative process.* Santa Barbara, CA: Clio Books.

Neumann, R. K., Jr. (1994). *Legal reasoning and legal writing: Structure, strategy and style* (2nd ed.). Boston: Little, Brown.

Nichols, C. A. (1974). *Nichols cyclopedia of legal forms annotated.* Chicago: Callaghan.

Nyberg, C., & Boast, C. (1984). *Subject compilations of state laws, 1979-1983: Research guide and annotated bibliography.* Westport, CT: Greenwood.

Rombauer, M. D. (1991). *Legal problem solving: Analysis, research and writing* (5th ed.). St. Paul, MN: West.

Shapo, H. S., Walter, M. R., & Fajans, E. (1995). *Writing and analysis in the law* (3rd ed.). New York: Foundation Press.

Squires, L. B. (1982). *Legal writing in a nutshell.* St. Paul, MN: West.

Statsky, W. P. (1993). *Legal research and writing: Some starting points* (4th ed.). St. Paul, MN: West.

Statsky, W. P., & Wernet, R. J., Jr., (1995). *Case analysis and fundamentals of legal writing* (4th ed.). St. Paul, MN: West.

Index

A.D.S. *(American Digest System)*, 19-20, 25, 71
A.L.R. *(American Law Reports)*, 10
A.L.R.-Fed. *(American Law Reports-Federal)*, 10
Acts and resolves. *See* Session laws
Administrative Procedure Act, 102
Advance Sheets, United States Code Service, 73
Am. Jur. 2d *(American Jurisprudence 2d)*, 10
American Digest System (A.D.S.), 19-20, 25, 71
American Jurisprudence 2d (Am. Jur. 2d), 10
American Jurisprudence Legal Forms, Second Edition, 6
American Law Reports (A.L.R.), 10
American Law Reports Digest, 10
American Law Reports-Federal (A.L.R.-Fed.), 10
American Law Reports-Federal Digest, 10
Appellate courts, 14, 67 (n11), 67 (n16)
Arizona Digest, 25
Atlantic Digest, 19
Atlantic Reporter, 22-24
Attorneys, as research consultants, 5-6

B.N.A. (Bureau of National Affairs), 18
Berring, R. C., 4
Bills, checking status of, 83
Bitner, H., 4
Black's Law Dictionary, 4
Bluebook, The: A Uniform System of Citation, 4, 67 (n1), 76, 98 (n2), 99 (n6)

Briefing cases, 25, 67 (n14)
Bureau of National Affairs (B.N.A.), 18
Bysiewicz, S., 4

C.C.H. (Commerce Clearing House), 18
C.F.R. *See Code of Federal Regulations* (C.F.R.)
C.J.S. *(Corpus Juris Secundum),* 10, 71
C.L.I. (Current Law Index), 9-10
California Digest 2d, 19
California Reporter, 16
Case law:
    case reporting systems, 14-20
    citation style, 20-22
    finding alternative citations, 22
    finding relevant cases, 25-27
    reading cases, 22-25
    restatements of, 10-11
Case reporting systems, 14-20
    digests, 18-20
    federal decisions, 16-18, 63
    state decisions, 14-16, 63-66
Century Digests, 20
Circuits, federal judicial, 17 (table)
Citation style:
    for cases, 20-22
    for federal administrative law, 108
    finding alternative case citations, 22
    for statutory material, 75-76
Code of Federal Regulations (C.F.R.), 109, 129 (n13)
    citation style, 108
    finding regulations, 105-107
    titles, 118-119
Codification Guides, 104-105
Cohen, M. L., 4
Commerce Clearing House (C.C.H.), 18

Computer-assisted research, x, 12
Congressional Index, 82
Congressional Information Service/Index, 79, 80, 82
Congressional Legislative Reporting Service, 78-79
Congressional Quarterly Weekly Report, 82-83
Congressional Record, 80, 81, 82
Consent decree, 67 (n12)
Constitutions, state, 72
Constitutions of the U.S.: National and State, 2d ed., 72
Corpus Juris Secundum (C.J.S.), 10, 71
Courts, rules for:
    federal courts, 74-75
    state courts, 72
Cumulative Index of Congressional Committee Hearings, 79
Current Law Index (C.L.I.)-Legal Resource Index (L.R.I.), 9-10

Decennial Digests, 20
Decisions and orders, federal, 107-108
Depository Library Act, 5
Dicta, 24
Digest of Public General Bills, 82
Digests, 11-12
    case law, 18-20
Directory of Uniform Acts and Codes Tables-Index, 71
Dunn, D. J., 4, 98 (n3)
Dunn, P., 18

Education Law Reporter, 18
Effective Legal Research, 4
Encyclopedias, legal, 10
Ending the research process, 12-13
Environmental Law Reporter, 18
Executive branches, 7-8

Fair Employment Law Reporter, 67 (n10)
Federal administrative law:
    citation style, 108
    mandated public access, 102-104
    other information sources, 109
    research tools for decisions and orders, 107-108
    research tools for rules and regulations, 104-107
Federal Banking Law Reporter, 67 (n10)
Federal judicial circuits, 17 (table)
Federal law. *See also* Federal administrative law
    administrative law, 102-109
    case law, 16-18, 63
    checking status of proposed legislation, 83
    finding statutes, 73-75, 98
    legislative materials, 98
    reporters, 63
    researching legislative history, 78-83
    service reporters, 122-128
    session laws, 98
Federal Practice and Procedure, 74
Federal Register, 109, 128 (n11)
    citation style, 108
    Codification Guides, 104-105
    and Freedom of Information Act, 102-104
Federal Reporter, 17
Federal Rules Decisions, 17
Federal Securities Law Reporter, 67 (n10)
Federal Supplement, 17, 67 (n10)
Finishing the research process, 12-13
Fisher, M. L., 77
Form books, 6
Freedom of Information Act, 101-104
Fundamentals of Legal Research, 4

Gelfand, A., 18
General Digest, The, 20
Gerstein, R. S., 18
Government Organization Manual, 104
Guide to State Legislative Materials, Fourth Edition, 77

Handbook of the National Conference of Commissioners on Uniform State Laws and Proceedings, 71
Harvard Law Review Association, 4
Hellebust, L., 77

INDEX

Hierarchy of laws, 7-8
History of legislation. See Legislative history
Holding, the, 24
House and Senate Documents, 80
House and Senate Journals, 80
How to Find the Law, 4
How to Use Shepard's Citations, 67 (n16)

I.L.P. (Index to Legal Periodicals), 9-10
Index to Legal Periodicals (I.L.P.), 9-10
Interstate statutory compacts, 71-72
Interstate Compacts and Agencies, 71-72

Jacobstein, J. M., 4, 98 (n3)
Judicial branches, 7-8
Judicial circuits, federal, 17 (table)

Key Number System (West):
  finding relevant cases, 25
  overview of, 18-19
  reading cases, 24

L.R.I. (Legal Resource Index), 9-10
Labor Cases, 18
Law digests, 11-12
Law libraries, 4-5
Law reviews, 9-10
Laws. *See* Case law; Legislative history; Session laws; Statutes
Lawyers Co-operative:
  Lawyer's Edition of the U.S. Supreme Court Reports, 10, 16-17
  United States Code Service, 73, 74, 81
Lawyer's Edition of the U.S. Supreme Court Reports, 10, 16-17
Legal encyclopedias, 10
Legal Research in a Nutshell, 4
Legal Resource Index (L.R.I.), 9-10
Legal Writing Style, 4
Legislative branches, 7-8
Legislative history, 76-83
  checking status of proposed legislation, 83
  finding federal materials, 78-83

finding state materials, 77
obtaining an existing history, 80-83
overview of, 76-77
LEXIS, x, 12
Library research, social sciences vs. law, 3
Lieberson, A. D., 6

Martindale-Hubbell Law Directory, 24
Mental health practitioners, legal issues' importance, ix
Mersky, R. M., 4, 98 (n3)
Miller, 74
Model Federal Jury Instructions: Criminal & Civil, 6
Monthly Catalog of U.S. Government Publications, 79, 80
Moore's Federal Practice, 74
Moore's Federal Practice Rules Pamphlet, 74

National Conference of Commissioners on the Uniform State Laws, 70-71
National Directory of State Agencies, The, 100
National Reporter Blue Book, 22
Nebraska Administrative Code, 101
New York Supplement, 16
North Western Digest, 19
Numerical Order of Bills and Resolutions Which Have Passed Either or Both House, and Bills Now Pending on the Calendar, 82

Obiter dictum, 24
Olson, K. C., 4
Opinions of the Attorney General of the United States, 109
Orders and decisions, federal, 107-108

Pacific Digest, 19
Practitioners, legal issues' importance, ix, 2
Price, M. O., 4
Primary sources, 7
Privacy Act of 1974, 104

Private vs. public laws, 98 (n3)
Product Liability Reporter, 67 (n10)
Public vs. private laws, 98 (n3)

Reading cases, 22-25
Reed v. State, 35-62
 Atlantic Reporter information, 22-24
 citation style, 20-22
 edited version of opinion, 35-62
 finding relevant cases, 25-27
References, 4, 130-132
Regions of West system, 16
Regulations, federal, 104-107
Remanding a case, 67 (n11)
Reporters:
 for federal cases, 16-18, 63
 service reporters, 122-128
 for state cases, 15-16, 63-66
Research consultants, attorneys as, 5-6
Researchers, legal issues' importance, 1-2
Resolves. *See* Statutes
Restatements of law, 10-11
Reviews, law, 9-10
Reynolds, W. L., 18
Richman, W. M., 18
Rules and regulations, federal, 104-107
Rules for courts:
 federal courts, 74-75
 state courts, 72

S.C.B. *(Supreme Court Bulletin),* 17
Sand, L. B., 6
Schuchman, P., 18
Scientists, legal issues' importance, ix
Secondary sources, 7
Service reporters, 122-128
Session laws, 68. *See also* Statutes
 federal legislative materials, 98
 state legislative materials, 93-97
Shepardizing, 26-27
Shepard's Acts and Cases by Popular Names: Federal and State, 69-70
Shepard's Citations, 22, 26-27
Shepard's Code of Federal Regulations Citations, 106
Shepard's Federal Energy Law Citations, 108

Shepard's Federal Labor Law Citations, 108
Shepard's Immigration and Naturalization Citations, 108
Shepard's Occupational Safety and Health Citations, 108
Shepard's United States Administrative Citations, 108, 109
Shepard's United States Patents and Trademarks Citations, 108
Slip laws, 68
Social science:
 legal issues' importance, ix
 research compared to legal research, 3
Sources, primary vs. secondary, 7
South Eastern Digest, 19
Southern Reporter, 2nd Series, 16
Southern Reporter, 16
Stare decisis, 14
State constitutions, 72
State law:
 administrative law, 100-102, 114-117
 case law, 14-16, 63-66
 checking status of proposed legislation, 83
 finding statutes, 70-72, 89-93
 legislative materials, 89-93
 reporters, 63-66
 researching legislative history, 77
 session laws, 68, 93-97, 98
State Legislative Sourcebook, 77
State-mandated public access, 100-102
Statutes, 68-76. *See also* Legislative history
 checking status of proposed legislation, 83
 citation style, 75-76
 federal legislative materials, 98
 finding, 68-75
 session laws, 68, 93-97, 98
 in state law, 70-72
 state legislative materials, 89-93
 uniformity, 70-71
Statutes at Large, 68, 71, 73, 98, 109
Stopping the research process, 12-13
Style of citations. *See* Citation style
Supplemental reading, 132
Supreme Court Bulletin (S.C.B.), 17
Supreme Court Reporter, 16-17

INDEX

Texts, 8-9
Trade Cases, 67 (n10)
Treatises, 8-9

U.L.A. *(Uniform Laws Annotated),* 71
U.S. Law Week (U.S.L.W.), 17, 67 (n9)
U.S. Statutes at Large, 68, 71, 73, 98, 109
U.S. Supreme Court Digest, Lawyer's Edition, 74
U.S.C. *See* United States Code (U.S.C.)
U.S.C.A. *(United States Code Annotated),* 72, 74, 81
U.S.C.C.A.N. *(United States Code Congressional and Administrative News),* 73, 79-80, 109
U.S.C.S. *(United States Code Service),* 73, 74, 82
U.S.L.W. *(U.S. Law Week),* 17, 67 (n9)
Uniform Laws Annotated (U.L.A.), 71
Uniformity, statutory, 70-71
United States Code Annotated, 73, 74, 81
United States Code Congressional and Administrative News (U.S.C.C.A.N.), 73, 79-80, 109
United States Code Service (U.S.C.S.), 73, 74, 81
United States Code (U.S.C.), 69, 74, 81
  Advance Sheets, 73
  titles, 120-121
United States Reports, 16-17
Unofficial reporters:
  service reporters, 122-128
  state decisions, 15-16, 63-66

Vacating an opinion, 67 (n11)

Weekly Compilation of Presidential Documents, 80, 109
Weihofen, H., 4
West system:
  American Digest System, 19-20, 25
  California Digest 2d, 19
  in case citations, 20
  Decennial Digests, 20
  digests, 18-20
  Education Law Reporter, 18
  Federal Reporter, 17
  Federal Rules Decisions, 17
  Federal Supplement, 17, 67 (n10)
  Key Number System, 18-19, 24, 25
  National Reporter system, 16
  Supreme Court Reporter, 16-17
  United States Code Annotated, 73, 74, 81
  United States Code Congressional and Administrative News, 73, 79-80, 109
WESTLAW, x, 12, 71
West's Legal Forms, Revised Second Edition, 6
Wright, N. D., 100

About the Authors

Roberta A. Morris received her PhD from the University of Nebraska-Lincoln's (UNL) Department of Psychology and her JD from its College of Law. She was one of the early students in the fledgling Law and Psychology Graduate Training Program at UNL. Her scholarly interests were in assessing the validity of assumptions underlying law and policies, particularly in reference to how they affect human behavior. She had authored several articles and chapters, and this volume was her first effort at writing a book-length manuscript. At the time of her death, she was in legal practice in Denver, CO, where she was tragically killed in an automobile accident before seeing the completion of her work.

Bruce D. Sales is Professor of Psychology, Psychiatry, Sociology, and Law at the University of Arizona. Having twice served as the President of the American Psychology-Law Society (1976-77 and 1985-86) and as the first editor of *Law and Human Behavior* and *Psychology, Public Policy and Law,* he is the recipient of the American Psychology-Law Society's Distinguished Contribution Award to Psychology and Law (1992); the American Psychological Association Division of Psychologists in Public Service Harold M. Hildreth Award for "exceptional dedication and achievement in promoting the public welfare" (1995); the State of Arizona Governor's Spirit of Excellence Award (1995); and the American Psychological Association's Award For Distinguished Professional Contributions To Public Service (1995). His recent books include *Mental Health and Law: Research, Policy and Services* (with S. Shah, in press); *Law, Mental Health, and Mental Disorder* (with D. Shuman, 1996); and *Psychology in Litigation and Legislation* (with G. VandenBos, 1994). As Dr. Morris's PhD advisor at UNL early in her career, he remained her colleague and friend until her untimely demise.

Daniel W. Shuman is Professor of Law at Southern Methodist University School of Law and adjunct Professor of Psychiatry at the University of Texas, Southwestern Medical School. He is the recipient of the American Psychiatric Association Manfred S. Guttmacher Award For Outstanding Contribution to Law and Psychiatry (1988). He has authored five books, including *Psychiatric and Psychological Evidence* (1986; 2nd ed., 1994); *Law, Mental Health and Mental Disorder* (with B. Sales, 1996); *Law and Mental Health Professionals* (1990); and *The Psychotherapist-Patient Privilege* (with Weiner, 1987), as well as more than 35 articles and chapters. He is a former chair of the Association of American Law Schools section on Law and Mental Disability and Law and Medicine.

APPLIED SOCIAL RESEARCH METHODS SERIES

Series Editors
LEONARD BICKMAN, Peabody College, Vanderbilt University, Nashville
DEBRA J. ROG, Vanderbilt University, Washington, DC

32. **APPLIED RESEARCH DESIGN**
    by TERRY E. HEDRICK,
    LEONARD BICKMAN,
    and DEBRA J. ROG
33. **DOING URBAN RESEARCH**
    by GREGORY D. ANDRANOVICH
    and GERRY RIPOSA
34. **APPLICATIONS OF CASE STUDY RESEARCH**
    by ROBERT K. YIN
35. **INTRODUCTION TO FACET THEORY**
    by SAMUEL SHYE
    and DOV ELIZUR
    with MICHAEL HOFFMAN
36. **GRAPHING DATA**
    by GARY T. HENRY
37. **RESEARCH METHODS IN SPECIAL EDUCATION**
    by DONNA M. MERTENS
    and JOHN A. McLAUGHLIN
38. **IMPROVING SURVEY QUESTIONS**
    by FLOYD J. FOWLER, Jr.
39. **DATA COLLECTION AND MANAGEMENT**
    by MAGDA STOUTHAMER-LOEBER
    and WELMOET BOK VAN KAMMEN
40. **MAIL SURVEYS**
    by THOMAS W. MANGIONE
41. **QUALITATIVE RESEARCH DESIGN**
    by JOSEPH A. MAXWELL
42. **ANALYZING COSTS, PROCEDURES, PROCESSES, AND OUTCOMES IN HUMAN SERVICES**
    by BRIAN T. YATES
43. **DOING LEGAL RESEARCH**
    by ROBERT A. MORRIS, BRUCE D. SALES,
    and DANIEL W. SHUMAN
44. **RANDOMIZED EXPERIMENTS FOR PLANNING AND EVALUATION**
    by ROBERT F. BORUCH
45. **MEASURING COMMUNITY INDICATORS**
    by PAUL J. GRUENEWALD,
    ANDREW J. TRENO, GAIL TAFF,
    and MICHAEL KLITZNER

Other volumes in this series are listed on the series page